TEXAS PRIDE

MW00717718

AP Wide World

Published by Triumph Books, Chicago.
Copyright © 2006 by Athlon Sports. All rights reserved.

Content packaged by Mojo Media, Inc.
Editor: Joe Funk
Creative Director: Jason Hinman

Athlon Sports
Editor: Rob Doster
Contributing Writer: Joseph Duarte
Photo Editor: Tim Clark

No part of this publication may be reproduced, stored in a retrieval system, or transmitted, in any form by any means, electronic, mechanical, photocopying, or otherwise, without prior written permission of the publisher, Triumph Books, 601 S. LaSalle St., Suite 500, Chicago, Illinois 60605.

Cover photos copyright AP Wide World
All photos copyright UT Sports Photos except where otherwise noted.

This book is available in quantity at special discounts for your group or organization.
For further information, contact:

Triumph Books
601 S. LaSalle St.
Suite 500
Chicago, Illinois 60605
Phone: (312) 939-3330
Fax: (312) 663-3557

Printed in the United States of America

AP Wide World

Contents

FOREWORD

I was watching the national champion Longhorn baseball team play last season when it occurred to me what a special fraternity the Texas Longhorn football program is. Coach Darrell Royal was at the baseball game, and everyone in the stands was interested in talking to him, even though he retired in 1976. There's a lot of pride in saying that I played for such a great coach and for a school like Texas, and it's a pride that all Longhorn fans share. That pride has only deepened in watching the exploits of the 2005 Longhorns.

All the athletes who were associated with Coach Royal at the time were living a dream, and it was a great opportunity. It's important that today's players understand how important it is to be a Longhorn and to make the most of it. Vince Young & Co. have done just that.

One of the greatest moves Coach Mack Brown has made was to reunite the members of the football family who have played for the University of Texas. He brought back the tradition, which has always been there but had slid back a little bit. That has helped build on the foundation and has made the family stronger. Being a Longhorn is a feeling of pride unlike any other.

Some of my greatest memories as a Longhorn include the opportunity to play in the Texas-Arkansas games and against Notre Dame in the 1970 Cotton Bowl. Notre Dame was coming out of retirement, so to speak, to play in the bowl game (the Irish hadn't played in a bowl since 1925) and their name was synonymous with college football back then. They were the only team you could watch on Sundays; the Fighting Irish's games were replayed on that day. So it was especially meaningful to win that game 21–17 in a thrilling comeback and complete an unbeaten National Championship season. Today, I'm delighted that the 2005 Longhorns will have similar memories to cherish.

I have great memories of my time at Texas, but what's especially amazing to me is how many people remember the things I did while I was a Longhorn. It was just a neat experience. As I have gotten older, I realize just how lucky I was and how everything fell into place for me. I got to meet President Nixon after the Arkansas game in 1969 and President Johnson after the Notre Dame game that year. Later on, I went to Las Vegas and had the fortune to meet Elvis backstage and Bill Medley of the Righteous Brothers. (Elvis said Texas deserved to beat Arkansas, while Bill Medley said he wanted Arkansas to win. I always was an Elvis fan!)

There is a lot of pride when you become a Longhorn. When you come to UT, you have access to a network of people for the rest of your life, whether you were a starter or not. When you go out to the business world, being a Longhorn means a lot. People always want to talk about my playing days and what's going on these days. My time at Texas opened several doors for me, and it continues to do so 30 years later.

I look back, and it all seems like it was a fairy tale or someone else's life. I'm thankful for the memories and everything UT has done for me. And today, I'm so proud of the 2005 Longhorns for adding a special chapter to the history of Texas football.

— **James Street**

One of the great moments in Texas football history. James Street confers with Darrell Royal on UT's game-winning drive in the 1970 Cotton Bowl victory over Notre Dame that punctuated a national championship season.

FROM THE EDITORS

The greatest game in history? With all that was on the line, it may well have been.

The greatest team in history? Let the discussion begin.

On a steamy night on the storied turf of the Rose Bowl, the 2005 Texas Longhorns kept their year-long date with destiny, finishing a 13–0 season for the ages with a game for all time.

One year ago, Vince Young stood on the same turf and vowed to return in January 2006 for the BCS championship game. Young was as good as his word. After a dominant regular season and an unstoppable march to the Big 12 title, Young and his Longhorn teammates put on quite possibly the most thrilling show in college football history in a 41–38 win over the two-time defending champion USC Trojans that colored the 2005 Championship burnt orange and white.

A season of unmatched excellence reached a stunning crescendo with a comeback victory that will live on in Longhorn lore for as long as Bevo prowls the sidelines and fans wave the Hook 'em sign. Texas' rally from a 38–26 deficit may have surprised many onlookers, but not those who have watched the Longhorns give a season-long lesson in heart.

Young may not own a Heisman, but he owns the Rose Bowl like it's his own personal playground. His 467 yards of total offense in an epic championship game performance put the perfect exclamation point on a season of invincibility, pun intended. And how appropriate it was that Young covered the final eight yards of the season with his legs, relegating the USC defense to the role of spectator, just as he did to defenses all season long.

And let's not forget the Longhorn defense. Virtually ignored heading into the Rose Bowl despite a dominant regular season, the Texas defenders smacked the Trojans all game long, then rose up and made the play of their lives, stuffing LenDale White on fourth-and-two with 2:09 left and giving Young a chance to work his magic.

Legendary college football announcer Keith Jackson correctly observed that this game and season were a validation of Mack Brown's program, and they restored Texas to its accustomed position atop the college football world.

A coach they said couldn't win the big one won the biggest one of all. And the Heisman runner-up took a back seat to no one on college football's biggest stage.

"There's a lot of passion and a lot of pride," Brown proclaimed from the podium after the game as he watched the jubilant celebration unfold in front of him.

The book is a celebration of that passion and pride. We hope you enjoy reading, as much we enjoyed documenting, the Longhorns' unforgettable 2005 championship season. ■

AP Wide World

Selvin Young celebrates his second quarter touchdown with teammate Quan Cosby as confident play set the tone for the Longhorns in the Rose Bowl.

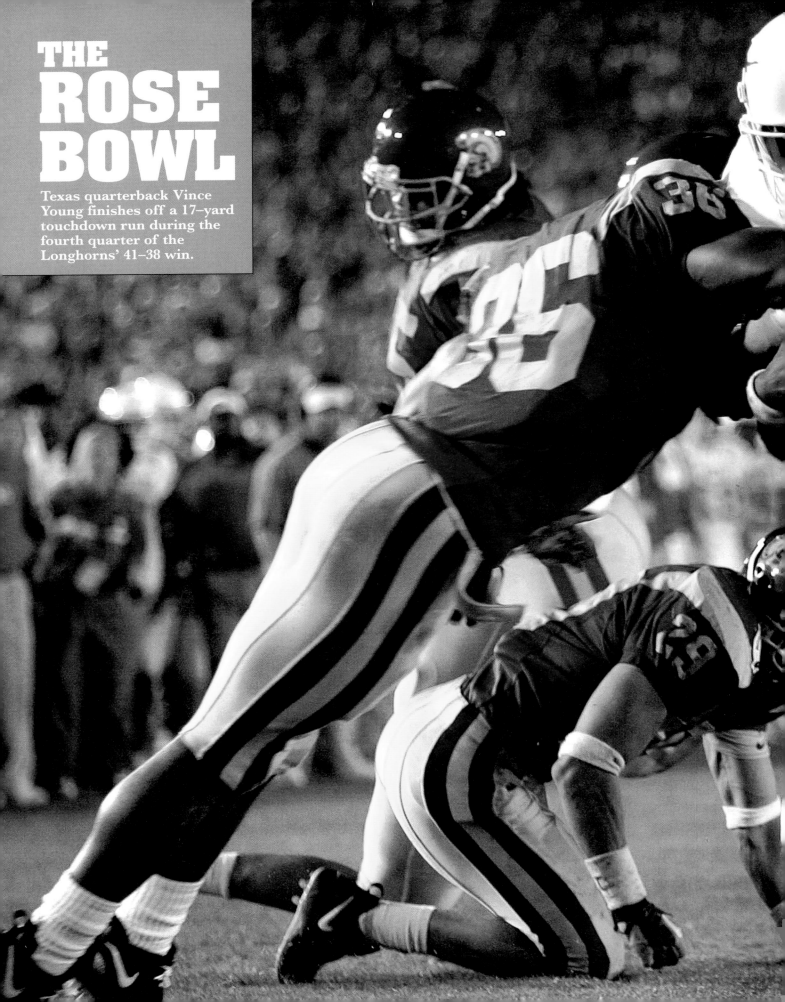

THE ROSE BOWL

Texas quarterback Vince Young finishes off a 17–yard touchdown run during the fourth quarter of the Longhorns' 41–38 win.

AP Wide World

INVINCIBLE YOUNG CONVINCES TROJANS

Texas 41, USC 38 • The Rose Bowl, Jan. 4, 2006

PASADENA, California – The theme for the month leading up to the Bowl Championship Series national title game was USC's pursuit of history.

As it turns out, the two-time defending national champions were chasing Vince Young.

And they never caught him.

So much for USC's 34-game winning streak. So much for USC's quest for an unprecedented third straight title.

After one of the greatest performances in college football history, there was only one way to truly describe Texas' dazzling junior quarterback: In-Vince-ible.

Young rushed for 200 yards, passed for 267 yards and scored the decisive 8-yard touchdown with 19 seconds left as the No. 2 Longhorns stunned USC, 41–38, before a crowd of 93,986 in the Rose Bowl.

"He's one of the great players to ever play college football," Texas coach Mack Brown said.

The Longhorns completed a 13–0 season and captured their first national championship since 1970, when legendary coach Darrell Royal stalked the sidelines. USC lost for the first time since a triple-overtime defeat to California on Sept. 27, 2003, and the loss denied the Trojans' bid to become the first team to win three consecutive national titles.

The meeting of the two most explosive offenses in Division I-A lived up to the hype with Texas and USC combining for 1,130 yards of total offense.

"If you have to hand it over and step aside for somebody, that's a heck of a team to do that for," Carroll said.

The Trojans didn't hand it over – Young ripped it from their grip with a furious 12-point, fourth-quarter rally for the ages. With Texas trailing 38–26, Young did the only thing he could do.

He improvised.

The Longhorns began their rally with Young's 17-yard touchdown run that narrowed the deficit to 38–33 with 4:03 remaining. USC attempted to run out the clock, but came up short when LenDale White, who rushed for 124 yards and three touchdowns, was stopped on a fourth-and-2 gamble by the Trojans.

"If we make a first, the game's over," Carroll said. "We'd seen what they'd done the series before. It didn't matter where they were going to start."

Texas took possession on their 44-yard line and Young marched them effortlessly down the field. Quan Cosby's only catch of the game was critical, a seven-yarder on third down that was aided by a facemask penalty against USC safety Darnell Bing.

Later in the drive, Young threw incomplete on first down, ran for five yards on second down and missed Limas Sweed, the hero in Texas' 25–22 Week 2 victory at Ohio State, in the back of the end zone on third down. Down to his last play, Young dropped back to pass, couldn't find any open receivers and instinctively took off to the

AP Wide World

Young scores the game-winning touchdown and etches his name in college football lore.

> ## "If you have to hand it over and step aside for somebody, that's a heck of a team to do that for."
>
> – USC Coach Pete Carroll

right side, where he high-stepped untouched eight yards into the end zone. He added the two-point conversion.

This is what Young meant by "Jordan Mode," which he defines as "the feeling of confidence when you know you're going to win the game and nobody can stop you."

Fittingly, Young's mother, Felicia, wore a shirt earlier in the day with his photo, his No. 10 and the slogan "The Legacy Continues."

Young finished with 467 all-purpose yards and three second-half touchdowns to earn Rose Bowl Most Valuable Player honors for the second straight year. In his previous trip to the Rose Bowl in 2005, Young had 372 all-purpose yards and five touchdowns as the Longhorns edged Michigan 38–37 on a field goal by Dusty Mangum as time expired.

"Do whatever it takes," said Young, who became the first player in NCAA history to rush for 1,000 yards (1,050) and pass for 3,000 yards (3,036) in a season.

At the Heisman Trophy presentation in early December, Young expressed his disappointment at losing to USC tailback Reggie Bush in a landslide. He promised to come out motivated for the national title game and "show the world how good a team the University of Texas is."

"He's a Heisman Trophy winner in my book," All-American safety Michael Huff said. "We knew when we needed a play he was going to get it."

For more than a month, the Longhorns had fielded questions about the 2005 Trojans place as one of the greatest teams ever in college football. ESPN even featured a series on SportsCenter during the weeks leading up to the Rose Bowl that favorably compared the 2005 USC team with some of the greatest in NCAA history.

What about the 2005 Longhorns?

"We don't have to be the greatest team of all-time," Brown told his team before the game, "just the greatest team (in the championship game)."

Things didn't go that smoothly for the Longhorns in the first half. Texas' special teams unit, one of the best in the nation during the regular season, struggled. Aaron Ross fumbled a punt after Texas had held the Trojans on their opening drive, the Longhorns failed to convert on a fourth-and-1, and David Pino missed an extra point.

USC uncharacteristically wasted three scoring opportunities in consecutive first half series: they were stuffed on a fourth-and-1; turned over the ball on Longhorns' 19 after an ill-advised lateral from Bush; and Matt Leinart's pass to Steve Smith in the end zone was intercepted by safety Michael Griffin on a spectacular grab, which prevented the Trojans from taking a 14–3 lead.

After that, the Longhorns surprised the Trojans by using a no-huddle offense and marched down the field to the USC 22. Young went 10 yards on an option keeper and (after his knee apparently touched the ground) pitched to roommate Selvin Young, who took it the final 12 yards for the touchdown and UT's first lead despite a missed extra point, 9–7.

On its next possession, Texas needed only four plays and 72 seconds to push the lead to 16–7, capped off by Ramonce Taylor's 30-yard touchdown run. USC threatened just before halftime and got as close as the UT 13-yard line before Frank Okam had back-to-back sacks to stall the drive and force the Trojans to settle for a career-long 43-yard field goal by Mario Danelo, which gave Texas a 16-

Safety Michael Griffin intercepts a pass from Trojan quarterback Matt Leinart during the second quarter.

AP Wide World

AP Wide World

AP Wide World

Young dives past USC's Scott Ware for a third-quarter touchdown.

10 halftime lead.

It was only the eighth time — but fifth this season — that USC had trailed at halftime during its 34-game winning streak.

Young, criticized prior to the season for his lack of accuracy as a passer, completed nine straight passes to begin the game and went 13-of-15 for 113 yards in the first half. For the game, Young completed 30-of-40 passes for 267 yards and did not throw an interception.

"He's an extraordinary football player," Carroll said.

But everyone knew a six-point halftime lead was nothing against the USC offense. Like each of the other times it had trailed, USC came roaring back. Leinart, the 2004 Heisman winner, led the Trojans to scores on their first four possessions of the second half.

Leinart completed his first nine passes to after the break and finished with 365 yards and one touchdown in his final collegiate game. He became only the second quarterback to throw for 300 yards against the Longhorns this season.

White, pounded the Longhorns up the middle for most of the game, scored on a 3-yard run early in the third quarter to give USC a 17–16 lead. But Texas promptly answered. Again running the hurry-up offense, Young marched the Longhorns on a seven-play, 80-yard drive that was capped off with a 14-yard run by Young.

White scored his third rushing touchdown of the game, giving him a school-record 52 for his career, on a 12-yard run with 4:07 remaining in the third quarter that allowed the Trojans to regain a 24-23 lead. White had also scored on runs of 4 and 3 yards in the first half.

The Longhorns threatened again as Young completed four passes on the next drive and broke loose for a 45-yard run. But Texas came away with no points on the drive when Pino missed wide right on a 31-yard field goal attempt to begin the fourth quarter.

Bush, expected to be the top overall pick by the Houston Texans in the NFL draft this year, broke

"He's a Heisman Trophy winner in my book. We knew when we needed a play he was going to get it."

– Michael Huff on Vince Young

loose for a 26-yard touchdown to give USC what appeared to be a comfortable 31–23 lead. Overall, the explosive Bush had a quiet game, rushing for 84 yards and adding six catches for 95 yards. He had only four touches in the second half.

Pino atoned for his earlier miss with a 34-yard field goal, but the Trojans took a seemingly insurmountable 38–26 lead with under seven minutes remaining on Leinart's 22-yard pass to Dwayne Jarrett, who caught the ball at the 2 and lunged into the end zone. Jarrett, who had only two catches in the first half, finished with 10 for 121 yards.

All of this action set the stage for Young. It would be his sixth career fourth-quarter comeback. And his best.

After Young scored on a 17-yard touchdown run that capped a brisk 69-yard drive, the Trojans moved the ball close to midfield and positioned themselves to run out the clock.

Things looked bleak for the Longhorns. The USC offense could move the ball almost at will all night, and the Longhorns had no answer for LenDale White, giving Carroll the confidence to go for it and end the game right then and there. But on that historic fourth-and-2 play, the gamble backfired when Huff stuffed White inches short of the first down marker.

Vince Young time.

"We want the ball in Vince's hands," Texas defensive tackle Rod Wright said. "I wasn't feeling nervous at all."

Young went 4-of-7 on the final drive, completing two passes to Brian Carter and one to Taylor and Cosby. Finally, on a broken play that will forever be etched in Longhorn lore, Young found none of his receivers open but plenty of running space to the right side. He dodged one final tackler at the 5-yard line and danced into the end zone.

"He's a fantastic player and he made the difference," Carroll said. "How classic was it that he ran it in on the last play?"

USC had one last chance. With the Trojans starting at their own 31, Bush grabbed a shovel pass from Leinart and sprinted 27 yards to the Texas 42. With only eight seconds remaining, Leinart was flushed out of the pocket, and his final desperation pass sailed high over Jarrett's head around the 25.

Just like that, there's a new king of college football. Brown won his first national championship. Texas had its first title in 36 years. And the Trojans' 34-game winning streak was no more.

"It's been a great run. We've done some special things," Bush said. "I don't think we should be ashamed about anything."

Young stood on the field in a sea of confetti while hearing chants of "One more year!" from the UT crowd. He kissed the crystal national championship trophy.

If Young returns for his senior season, the Longhorns will have a shot at the school record of 30 straight victories, and Young will become the frontrunner for the Heisman.

"We'll be back," he said. "Wherever they play this game next year, we'll be back." ▪

AP Wide World

2005 PRESEASON

As summer wore on, expectations in Austin were soaring along with the temperatures. Here, we present Athlon Sports' preseason assessment of the 2005 Longhorns.

TEXAS LONGHORNS

National Forecast: 6 | **Big 12 South Prediction: 2nd**

Before Texas left on its trip to USC to play Michigan in the 2005 Rose Bowl, coach Mack Brown told his team to take mental notes.

From the practices at the Home Depot Center in Carson, Calif., to the trip to Disneyland, to the media demands, to the feel of the Rose Bowl's grass turf, Brown wanted nothing to be lost, especially among his returning players. Picturing life in Pasadena, where this season's BCS national title game will be played, is the first step toward returning, Brown reasoned.

"The message we're sending to our team in everything we do — from our off-season workouts to spring practice to the fall — is we want to go back to the Rose Bowl, and we want to win," Brown says.

The Longhorns won their first BCS bowl game by beating Michigan 38–37 on a last-second field goal as quarterback Vince Young became a national star. Young's dominating performance — four rushing TDs and one passing — is a big reason Texas is a sexy pick to overcome the losses of running back Cedric Benson and linebacker Derrick Johnson and challenge for a national title.

The Longhorns have their best offensive line since Brown arrived as coach eight years ago. On defense, there is depth on the line and in the secondary but big questions at outside linebacker.

Quarterbacks

Young has more tools to work with than any college quarterback should be allowed. He's got the swivel and speed of a running back and a 6'5" frame to look over linemen in the passing game. He's even got a former NFL co-MVP mentor in Tennessee Titans quarterback Steve McNair, who went to college at Alcorn State with Young's uncle, Ivory Young.

"Vince wants to be the best," says McNair, who attended UT's spring game in April. "He's shown me he's willing to make the sacrifices and do the little things to get there."

Young is throwing with more confidence because he is more familiar with the offense, even though he has the same three-quarters delivery.

Young's backup, senior Matt Nordgren, is untested.

Running Backs

Cedric Benson is gone. The future now belongs to fourth-year junior Selvin Young, sophomore Ramonce Taylor and possibly a true freshman such as Jamaal Charles or Henry Melton. Taylor, who is slight (5'11", 195) but fast, emerged from spring practice as a surefire tailback after bouncing between running back and receiver. Young missed spring practice while recovering from ankle surgery and working on his academics.

Young, who also happens to be best friends with Vince Young, is the most experienced running back on the team, having rushed for 661 yards and 10 touchdowns on 132 carries (5.0 ypc) over three seasons. But Taylor's outstanding spring means there's no guarantee Young will be the starter in the opener.

NUMBERS GAME

33 UT's leading receiver Tony Jeffery had 33 catches last season, marking the first time since 1997 that Texas didn't have a receiver with at least 40 catches.

Receivers

The Longhorns are desperate for their young talent to grow up quickly. Otherwise, senior tight end David Thomas could become the first non-wide-out to lead the team in catches and receiving yards since 1992.

Limas Sweed is the most experienced wideout on the team. Sweed, the projected starter at split end, has all the physical tools to be a go-to guy but has lacked consistency and a killer instinct. At flanker, freshman Jordan Shipley, who redshirted last season after tearing knee ligaments in the

Tim Clark/Athlon Sports

Post-Spring Analysis

Keys to a National Title

During spring practice, Texas began working on schemes for its game at Ohio State on Sept. 10. Not a bad idea considering the Buckeyes have arguably the most dangerous player in college football in Ted Ginn Jr. UT's special teams were leaky late last season, and Ginn will expose any weaknesses there. Ohio State will also have a veteran linebacking corps chasing Vince Young around. A victory over the Buckeyes in Columbus would solidify the Horns as national title contenders and give them momentum for the Oklahoma game in Dallas on Oct. 8. OU has beaten the Longhorns the last five years by an average of 27 points, helping keep UT from earning a national title shot or even from winning a Big 12 title under Mack Brown. With OU losing numerous key starters, Texas has its best chance to win the Red River Shootout in a while.

2005 Schedule

S. 3	UL Lafayette	W
S. 10	**at Ohio State**	*
S. 17	Rice	W
O. 1	at Missouri	W
O. 8	**#Oklahoma**	*
O. 15	Colorado	W
O. 22	Texas Tech	W
O. 29	at Oklahoma State	W
N. 5	at Baylor	W
N. 12	Kansas	W
N. 25	at Texas A&M	W
	#Dallas, TX	

*Games in **bold** represent games crucial to the season.
W or L indicates a projected win or loss.

Cedric Griffin: Has started 31 games in his Texas career

Tim Clark/Athlon Sports

Aaron Harris

RISING STAR

Redshirt freshman **Jordan Shipley** was arguably the best receiver in fall camp last season before tearing knee ligaments and having to sit out 2004. In practice, he is the team's best route runner and rarely drops a pass. If high school production is any indication (264 catches for 5,424 yards and 73 TDs at Burnet High School), Shipley will become a star this season.

preseason, has impressed coaches and should develop into a solid contributor this season.

Offensive coordinator Greg Davis wants to throw deep more this season by using play-action.

Offensive Linemen

Texas has four returning starters on the line, including all-star candidates in left tackle Jonathan Scott and right tackle Justin Blalock. Left guard Kasey Studdard proved to be one of the top newcomers on the team last season, and right guard Will Allen is an aggressive run blocker. Texas lost only center Jason Glynn from last year's line starters and has a ready replacement in Lyle Sendlein.

Defensive Linemen

Texas hasn't had a decent four-man pass rush or a double-digit sacker since Aaron Humphrey (10) in 1999. New defensive ends coach Oscar Giles, who led Texas in sacks in 1988 and 1989,

thinks that will change this season. He makes his players run if they don't record at least five sacks during scrimmage periods in practice. Giles also feels he has emerging stars at end in Tim Crowder, Mike Williams and Brian Orakpo.

"We are going to get to the quarterback this season," Giles says.

There is depth at defensive tackle thanks to seniors Rod Wright and Larry Dibbles, sophomore Frank Okam and incoming freshman Roy Miller. In obvious passing situations, UT will consider moving ends Brian Robison and Crowder to tackle and putting Williams and Orakpo at ends to get the four best pass rushers on the field.

Linebackers

This is the team's biggest question mark heading into the 2005 season. Butkus Award winner Derrick Johnson meant more to the Longhorns than his 130 tackles and an NCAA record nine forced fumbles last season.

Johnson's confidence and swagger, which rubbed off on players such as senior middle linebacker Aaron Harris, will be missed the most. Harris recorded 118 tackles last season (including 10 for a loss) in a breakout year and will need to pick up where he left off in the Rose Bowl, a game in which he had a team-leading nine tackles.

The battle to replace Johnson at weak-side

linebacker will be waged between sophomore Robert Killebrew and redshirt freshman Rashad Bobino, who keeps making plays. The leading candidate to play strong-side linebacker is junior Eric Foreman, who played linebacker as a freshman before switching to quarterback last season.

Defensive Backs

The secondary is loaded with depth, but it failed to come up with many interceptions last season (13).

Coaches are hoping playmaking will come with experience. Senior right cornerback Cedric Griffin has started 31 games and has been steady if not spectacular. Junior left cornerback Tarell Brown tied with Griffin and senior strong safety Michael Huff for the team lead in interceptions last season with two.

Huff is arguably the team's best cover man but plays safety because he's the best quarterback in the secondary. Michael Griffin will replace Phillip Geiggar at free safety.

Specialists

Rose Bowl hero Dusty Mangum has moved on, leaving the field goal chores to senior kicker David Pino, who is 3-of-4 on field goal attempts with a long of 39 yards. Punter Richmond McGee was a weapon at times last season, although his short kickoffs late in the season led to long returns that nearly proved costly in victories over Oklahoma State and Michigan.

Selvin Young and Taylor should be threats to score on kick and punt returns this season.

Key Longhorns

Vince Young, QB
Not only an All-America-type talent but a solid leader as well.

David Thomas, TE
Smart, versatile player who gives the offense a big dose of toughness.

Jonathan Scott, OL
Should be the best lineman on one of the best O-lines in the country.

Rod Wright, DT
The leader of the defense turned down the NFL for a chance at a title.

Aaron Harris, LB
Had a coming-out party last season with 118 tackles.

Key Losses

Cedric Benson, RB
Hard to replace his 1,834 rushing yards and 19 rushing TDs last season.

Derrick Johnson, LB
It will be his swagger that is most missed.

Phillip Geiggar, S
Underrated player and leader who just made plays and sure tackles.

Chance Mock, QB
Was one of the best backups in the nation.

Will Matthews, FB
Without him, Texas' ability to run out of a two-back set could be limited.

Head Coach: Mack Brown • Record at School: 70–19 (7 years) • Career Record: 156–93–1 (21 years) • Offensive Coordinator: Greg Davis
Defensive Coordinators: Duane Akina/Gene Chizik • Austin, Texas • Royal-Texas Memorial Stadium (80,082)

2005 Texas Roster

Quarterbacks

#	Name	POS	HT	WT	CL	Hometown
25	McCoy, Mark	QB	6'2"	185	Jr.	Dallas, TX
13	McCoy, Matthew	QB	6'3"	195	Jr.	Dallas, TX
7	Nordgren, Matt	QB	6'5"	235	Sr.	Dallas, TX
14	Torres, Freddy	QB	6'1"	190	Fr.	Pecos, TX
10	Young, Vince	QB	6'5"	230	Jr.	Houston, TX
16	Zepeda, Gilbert	QB	6'0"	186	So.	West Texas City, TX

Running Backs

#	Name	POS	HT	WT	CL	Hometown
12	Areias, Sam	RB	5'7"	210	Sr.	Los Banos, CA
31	Ballew, Scott	RB	5'11"	180	Fr.	Austin, TX
23	Carvajal, Jaime	RB	5'4"	147	So.	Southlake, TX
46	Hall, Ahmard	FB	5'11"	235	Sr.	Angleton, TX
29	Hofer, Matthew	RB	6'6"	185	So.	Dallas, TX
33	Houston, Michael	RB	5'11"	227	Fr.	Denver, CO
32	Myers, Marcus	RB	6'3"	250	Jr.	Austin, TX
3	Ogbonnaya, Chris	RB	6'1"	215	Fr.	Missouri City, TX
54	Taylor, Michael	FB/LB	5'11"	219	Fr.	Austin, TX
11	Taylor, Ramonce	RB	5'11"	195	So.	Temple, TX
22	Young, Selvin	RB	6'0"	210	Jr.	Houston, TX

Receivers

#	Name	POS	HT	WT	CL	Hometown
82	Aune, Coy	WR	6'2"	186	So.	Austin, TX
2	Carter, Brian	WR	5'11"	185	Sr.	The Woodlands, TX
17	Chareunsab, Xang	WR	5'8"	155	So.	Houston, TX
1	Gatewood, Tyrell	TE/WR	6'2"	210	So.	Tyler, TX
23	Hardy, Myron	WR	6'2"	210	So.	Austin, TX
83	Hogan, Steven	TE	6'5"	255	So.	Sugar Land, TX
9	Jones, Nate	WR	6'2"	190	So.	Texarkana, TX
89	Kendall, Daniel	WR	6'2"	185	Fr.	Houston, TX
41	Logan, Matt	WR	5'11"	156	Sr.	Houston, TX
85	Peters, Christoph	WR	6'3"	207	Fr.	Aachen, Greece
6	Pittman, Billy	WR	6'0"	195	So.	Cameron, TX
86	Portley, Kirby	TE	6'2"	215	Sr.	Kilgore, TX
8	Shipley, Jordan	WR	6'0"	184	Fr.	Burnet, TX
4	Sweed, Limas	WR	6'5"	215	So.	Washington, TX
27	Tefteller, Clayton	WR	6'0"	175	Jr.	Gilmer, TX
16	Thomas, David	TE	6'3"	245	Sr.	Wolfforth, TX
87	Tweedie, Neale	TE	6'5"	267	Jr.	Lucas, TX
86	Ullman, Peter	TE	6'4"	252	Fr.	Austin, TX
84	Walker, George	WR	6'3"	205	Fr.	Houston, TX

Offensive Linemen

#	Name	POS	HT	WT	CL	Hometown
72	Allen, Will	G	6'6"	315	Sr.	Houston, TX
63	Blalock, Justin	T	6'4"	329	Jr.	Plano, TX
55	Cannon, Matthew	OL/LS	6'2"	215	Jr.	The Woodlands, TX
55	Dockery, Cedric	G	6'4"	325	Fr.	Garland, TX
70	Dolan, Greg	T	6'7"	290	Fr.	Austin, TX
51	Garcia, Mike	G	6'3"	315	Sr.	Houston, TX
67	Griffin, Dallas	C	6'4"	280	So.	Katy, TX
79	Hills, Tony	T	6'6"	295	So.	Houston, TX
73	Scott, Jonathan	T	6'7"	310	Sr.	Dallas, TX
62	Sendlein, Lyle	C	6'5"	305	Jr.	Scottsdale, AZ
64	Studdard, Kasey	G	6'3"	295	Jr.	Lone Tree, CO
77	Thornton, Kyle	G	6'4"	320	So.	Dallas, TX
74	Ulatoski, Adam	T	6'8"	285	Fr.	Southlake, TX
66	Valdez, Brett	C	6'4"	305	Jr.	Brownwood, TX
78	Winston, William	T	6'7"	350	Sr.	Houston, TX

Defensive Linemen

#	Name	POS	HT	WT	CL	Hometown
80	Crowder, Tim	DE	6'4"	255	Jr.	Tyler, TX
92	Dibbles, Larry	DT	6'2"	285	Sr.	Lancaster, TX
58	Hand, Josh	DE	6'4"	253	Fr.	Henderson, NV
99	Jakes, Kaelen	DE	6'3"	270	Sr.	Valencia, CA
91	Janszen, Tully	DT	6'3"	280	Jr.	Keller, TX
96	Lokey, Derek	DT	6'2"	275	So.	Denton, TX
76	Marshall, Thomas	DT	6'6"	297	So.	Dallas, TX
94	Martin, Marco	DT	6'3"	355	Jr.	Mesquite, TX
97	Okam, Frank	DT	6'5"	315	So.	Dallas, TX
98	Orakpo, Brian	DE	6'4"	238	Fr.	Houston, TX
39	Robison, Brian	DE	6'3"	267	Jr.	Splendora, TX
61	Solis, Jaicus	DT	6'4"	250	Jr.	San Angelo, TX
81	Williams, Mike	DE	6'3"	240	Jr.	Lindale, TX
90	Wright, Rodrique	DT	6'5"	305	Sr.	Houston, TX

Linebackers

#	Name	POS	HT	WT	CL	Hometown
44	Bobino, Rashad	LB	5'11"	235	Fr.	West Texas City, TX
35	Bondy, Todd	LB	6'0"	206	So.	Southlake, TX
43	Campbell, Jeremy	LB	6'2"	220	Fr.	Richardson, TX
33	Derry, Scott	LB	6'3"	230	So.	Pearland, TX
21	Foreman, Eric	LB	6'4"	230	Jr.	Corrigan, TX
49	Hall, Eric	LB	6'2"	245	Sr.	Clarksville, TN
2	Harris, Aaron	LB	6'0"	235	Sr.	Mesquite, TX
30	Johnson, Braden	LB	6'1"	205	Sr.	Euless, TX
40	Killebrew, Robert	LB	6'2"	225	So.	Spring, TX
45	Redwine, Nic	LB	6'3"	225	Fr.	Tyler, TX
48	Schuldes, Roberto	LB	6'2"	200	Fr.	Modesto, CA
50	Tiemann, Luke	LB	6'2"	219	So.	Pflugerville, TX

Defensive Backs

#	Name	POS	HT	WT	CL	Hometown
5	Brown, Tarell	CB	6'0"	185	Jr.	Mesquite, TX
28	Foster, Brandon	CB	5'9"	180	So.	Arlington, TX
8	Griffin, Cedric	CB	6'2"	193	Sr.	San Antonio, TX
26	Griffin, Marcus	S	6'0"	190	So.	Austin, TX
27	Griffin, Michael	S	6'0"	200	Jr.	Austin, TX
7	Huff, Michael	S/CB	6'1"	205	Sr.	Irving, TX
1	Jackson, Erick	CB	6'2"	185	So.	Cedar Hill, TX
4	Kelson, Drew	DB	6'2"	210	So.	Houston, TX
21	Meijer, Karim	DB	5'10"	198	Sr.	Katy, TX
18	Melton, Matt	S	6'0"	210	Jr.	Flint, TX
24	Moench, Ryan	DB	6'0"	174	Fr.	Austin, TX
29	Palmer, Ryan	DB	5'10"	182	Fr.	Arlington, TX
36	Ray, James	DB	5'9"	190	Sr.	Hewitt, TX
31	Ross, Aaron	CB	6'1"	189	Jr.	Tyler, TX
42	Stavig, Cody	DB	5'10"	195	Sr.	Clackamas, OR
9	Tatum, Bobby	DB	6'0"	190	So.	Fort Worth, TX

Specialists

#	Name	POS	HT	WT	CL	Hometown
97	Johnson, Greg	P/K	6'1"	195	Jr.	Lilburn, GA
35	McGee, Richmond	P/K	6'4"	203	Sr.	Garland, TX
43	Moore, Justin	K	6'2"	185	Fr.	Houston, TX
37	Phillips, Kyle	K	5'11"	190	Sr.	Cypress, TX
15	Pino, David	K	5'8"	180	Sr.	Wichita Falls, TX

Projected Depth Chart

Offense (7)

FL	8 Jordan Shipley (Fr.)	9	Nate Jones (So.)
SE	**4 Limas Sweed (So.)**	23	Myron Hardy (Jr.)
TE	**16 David Thomas (Sr.)**	87	Neale Tweedie (Jr.)
LT	**73 Jonathan Scott (Sr.)**	79	Tony Hills (So.)
LG	**64 Kasey Studdard (Jr.)**	77	Kyle Thornton (So.)
C	62 Lyle Sendlein (Jr.)	66	Brett Valdez (Jr.)
RG	**72 Will Allen (Sr.)**	51	Mike Garcia (Sr.)
RT	**63 Justin Blalock (Jr.)**	78	William Winston (Sr.)
QB	**10 Vince Young (Jr.)**	7	Matt Nordgren (Sr.)
FB	**46 Ahmard Hall (Sr.)**	32	Marcus Myers (Jr.)
RB	22 Selvin Young (Jr.)	11	Ramonce Taylor (So.)

Defense (9)

DE	81 Mike Williams (Jr.)	39	**Brian Robison (Jr.)**
DT	**92 Larry Dibbles (Sr.)**	97	Frank Okam (So.)
DT	**90 Rod Wright (Sr.)**		Roy Miller (Fr.)
DE	**80 Tim Crowder (Jr.)**	98	Brian Orakpo (Fr.)
SLB	**21 Eric Foreman (Jr.)**	49	**Eric Hall (Sr.)**
MLB	**2 Aaron Harris (Sr.)**	33	Scott Derry (So.)
WLB	40 Robert Killebrew (So.)	44	Rashad Bobino (Fr.)
CB	**8 Cedric Griffin (Sr.)**	28	Brandon Foster (So.)
CB	**5 Tarell Brown (Jr.)**	31	Aaron Ross (Jr.)
SS	**7 Michael Huff (Sr.)**	9	Bobby Tatum (So.)
FS	27 Michael Griffin (Jr.)	18	Matt Melton (Jr.)

Special Teams

K	15 David Pino (Sr.)	KR	22 Selvin Young (Jr.)
P	35 Richmond McGee (Sr.)	PR	11 Ramonce Taylor (So.)

(#) indicates number of returning starters
BOLD indicates returning starters

2004 Individual Stats

Passing	Att.	Comp.	Pct.	Yds	TD	Int.
V. Young*	250	148	59.2	1849	12	11
C. Mock	21	9	42.9	79	0	0

Rushing	Att.	Yds.	Avg.	TD	YPG
C. Benson	326	1834	5.6	19	152.8
V. Young*	167	1079	6.5	14	89.9
R. Taylor*	28	284	10.1	1	28.4

Receiving	Rec.	Yds.	Avg.	Long	TD
T. Jeffery	33	437	13.2	46	3
B. Scaife	26	348	13.4	30	2
D. Thomas*	25	430	17.2	49	5

Tackles	Interceptions	Sacks	Tackles/Loss
D. Johnson, 130	M. Huff, 2*	T. Crowder, 4.5*	D. Johnson, 19
A. Harris, 118*	C. Griffin, 2*		A. Robison, 14*
M. Huff, 73*	T. Brown, 2*		

* Returning Player

Justin Blalock

2004 Results — 11–1 (7–1 Big 12)

Date	Opponent	Result	Score	Att.
S. 4	North Texas	W	65– 0	82,956
S. 11	at Arkansas	W	22–20	75,761
S. 25	Rice	W	35–13	82,931
O. 2	Baylor	W	44–14	82,626
O. 9	#Oklahoma	L	0–12	79,587
O. 16	Missouri	W	28–20	82,981
O. 23	at Texas Tech	W	51–21	55,413
O. 30	at Colorado	W	31– 7	51,751
N. 6	Oklahoma State	W	56–35	83,181
N. 13	at Kansas	W	27–23	38,714
N. 26	Texas A&M	W	26–13	83,891
J. 1	%Michigan	W	38–37	93,468
	#Dallas, TX			
	%Rose Bowl			

Scouting the Longhorns

Michael Huff

Big 12 coaches size up Texas: "This program has as much talent as any in the nation. They don't get the credit they deserve, but they can't seem to get over that hump. Until they do, Mack Brown will have his doubters. ... When you face the Longhorns, I think the first thing that comes to mind is the word 'athleticism.' No matter who leaves in a particular year Coach (Mack) Brown and his staff do an excellent job of bringing in some of the nation's best athletes. This year is no different. You look at who they are losing — Derrick Johnson, Cedric Benson, Bo Scaife, etc. — and you are tempted to think, 'Wow, they are really going to be hurting. But then look who they have coming back: Vince Young, Limas Sweed, Justin Blalock, Jonathan Scott, Rodrique Wright and so forth. It's a really impressive collection of athletes, and I think much of the country saw that in the Rose Bowl. That may have been a scary preview of things to come. Vince Young came into that game as a scrambler, but he left it as a dual-threat guy, who can obviously be an outstanding down-the-field thrower. Texas' receivers are just going to get better, as well, and the tight end, David Thomas, is a real load."

Outside the Huddle

Coaching change Defensive coaches Greg Robinson (Syracuse) and Dick Tomey (San Jose State) both left Texas after one season to take head coaching jobs. That's fine with Mack Brown, who is now only interested in hiring coordinators who aspire to run their own programs, such as Gene Chizik. They have energy and hunger that is contagious, Brown says.

Road warriors Texas has won 16 of its last 17 Big 12 road games and is 20–4 in league road contests under Mack Brown.

Foreman to the rescue Strong-side linebacker Eric Foreman raised a lot of eyebrows when he took himself out of a starting position on defense last season to become a fourth-string quarterback. His return to defense this season is a key because Texas lacks depth at linebacker, and Foreman is the most athletic player at the position.

Young's turning point The turning point in Vince Young's ascent at quarterback is easily traced to the Missouri game of last season. Young threw two early interceptions before taking a hit to the sternum and leaving the game. Young was cleared to return in the third quarter, but Mack Brown stuck with backup Chance Mock. Young took the snub as a challenge. He went back to his apartment and watched hours of videotape of himself playing free and easy in high school. Ever since, Young has been on a tear.

2005 Signees

Christopher Brown   LB   6'3"   210   **Texarkana, TX**
Named District 12 Class 4A Defensive Player of the Year and second-team All-State by TSWA. Recorded 119 tackles and 25 sacks as a senior; 103 tackles, 16 sacks and eight fumble recoveries as a junior.

Jamaal Charles   RB   6'1"   190   **Port Arthur, TX**
Named first-team Class 5A All-State by The AP and Offensive MVP by Houston Chronicle. Rushed for 2,056 yards and 25 TDs as a senior; 2,051 yards and 25 TDs as a junior. Named Parade All-American. Participated in U.S. Army All-American Bowl.

Quan Cosby   WR   5'11"   190   **Mart, TX**
Signed with Texas in 2001, but elected to play minor league baseball for the Angels. Named USA Today second-team All-USA at QB in 2000. Named 2A Texas Offensive Player of the Year, recording 3,329 yards of total offense and 42 TDs as a senior. Also ran track in HS, winning Class 2A state championships in 100 meters and 200 meters in 2001.

Jermichael Finley   WR   6'5"   220   **Diboll, TX**
Named first-team Class 3A All-State by TSWA and second-team Class 3A All-State by The AP. Recorded 878 receiving yards and 10 TDs, averaging 101 snaps per game as a senior. Also an all-state basketball player who averaged 24 points and 20 rebounds in 22 games as a senior.

Chris Hall   OL   6'4"   285   **Irving, TX**
Recorded 115 pancake blocks in 11 games as a senior; 125 pancake blocks in 14 games as a junior. Brother, Zach, plays LB at Arkansas Tech.

Michael Houston   RB   6'0"   230   **Denver, CO**
Rushed for 1,414 yards and 23 TDs as a senior. Captain of HS speech and debate team. Founder of group, "Young People Against Violence."

Aaron Lewis   DE   6'4"   270   **Albuquerque, NM**
Named New Mexico Gatorade Player of the Year and Parade All-American. Recorded 93 tackles, 17 sacks, three blocked punts, two safeties and one fumble recovery for a TD as a senior. Set state-record with 25.5 sacks as a junior. Played in U.S. Army All-American Bowl.

Colt McCoy   QB   6'3"   190   **Tuscola, TX**
Named Class 2A Offensive MVP and first-team Class 2A All-State by The AP following junior and senior seasons. Threw for 3,806 yards and 47 TDs; rushed for 541 yards and seven TDs as a senior. Threw for 3,939 yards and a single-season Class 2A state-record 50 TDs as a junior.

Henry Melton   RB   6'3"   270   **Grapevine, TX**
Named USA Today second-team All-USA. Rushed for 800 yards and eight TDs as a senior; 800 yards and 12 TDs as a junior. Lived in Japan as a child. Uncle, Ray Crockett, played 14 seasons in the NFL, winning back-to-back Super Bowls with the Denver Broncos.

Roy Miller   DT   6'2"   300   **Killeen, TX**
Participated in U.S. Army All-American Bowl, where he was named MVP of practice. He then finished second for MVP of the game, after registering two sacks in the contest. Recorded 111 tackles, 17 tackles for a loss, 10 sacks and one fumble recovery returned for a TD as a senior.

Roddrick Muckleroy   LB   6'2"   230   **Hallsville, TX**
Named first-team Class 4A All-State by The AP and TSWA as a senior. Recorded 104 tackles, 12 tackles for a loss and four sacks as a senior.

Ishie Oduegwu   ATH   5'10"   185   **Denton, TX**
Named first-team Class 5A All-State by The AP and TSWA as a senior. Recorded 167 tackles, 20 tackles for a loss and five INTs as a senior; with 148 tackles, two INTs and two punts returned for TDs as a junior.

Charlie Tanner   OL   6'4"   285   **Austin, TX**
Named second-team Class 5A All-State, recording 74 pancake blocks as a senior. Named Anderson HS Trojans Offensive Player of the Year and served as team captain during his junior and senior seasons.

Jerrell Wilkerson   RB   5'8"   180   **San Antonio, TX**
Named first-team Class 5A All-State by The AP and TSWA as a senior. Rushed for San Antonio city-record 7,249 yards and 110 TDs during career. Rushed for 2,501 yards and 47 TDs, with four kickoff return TDs and two punt return TDs as a senior. Cousin, Ronnie Lott, was an All-American safety at USC before playing 14 seasons in the NFL, where he went to 10 Pro Bowls and won four Super Bowls with the 49ers.

Class Notes

Mack Brown normally locks up his commitments in recruiting well before national signing day but went to the wire for two highly touted prospects — quarterback Ryan Perrilloux of Reserve, La., and tight end Martellus Bennett of Alief Taylor. Brown admitted after Perrilloux signed with LSU and Bennett signed with Texas A&M that he was "snookered" — especially by Perrilloux, who remained committed to Texas right up until signing his letter of intent to LSU. Brown has since said he won't allow Texas to remain the choice of a player who wants to turn recruiting into a spectacle.

Texas needed help at quarterback, running back, linebacker and defensive tackle and filled most of those needs. Brown wanted two quarterbacks in this recruiting class but ended up with only one — Colt McCoy of Tuscola Jim Ned. At running back, Jamaal Charles of Port Arthur Memorial, Henry Melton of Grapevine, Michael Houston of Denver (Colo.) Montbello and Jerrell Wilkerson of San Antonio Clark will battle in fall camp for a chance to play this season. Charles is quick and elusive, Melton and Houston are power backs, while Wilkerson is a speed back. Texas hopes it has found immediate help at receiver from Quan Cosby, who initially signed to play at Texas in 2001 before pursuing pro baseball with the Angels' organization.

Defensive tackle Roy Miller of Killeen Shoemaker also has a chance to play immediately. Defensive end Aaron Lewis of Albuquerque (N.M.) La Cueva is a *Parade* All-American who might find it hard to get on the field this season because of the depth at end. At linebacker, Roddrick Muckleroy of Hallsville and Christopher Brown of Texarkana appear to be players who can help, if not this year then next.

Recruiting Breakdown

By Position		By State	
Running Backs	4	Texas	12
Defensive Linemen	2	Colorado	1
Linebackers	2	New Mexico	1
Offensive Linemen	2		
Wide Receivers	2		
Athletes	1		
Quarterbacks	1		

Spotlight on...Henry Melton

Incoming freshman Henry Melton of Grapevine is a 6'3", 270-pound ... running back.

He may not last there for long, or he may. His uncle is Ray Crockett, who played 14 years in the NFL with Detroit, Denver and Kansas City. Crockett, who co-captained Denver's back-to-back Super Bowl teams in 1997 and 1998, believes Melton will be a defensive end in the NFL one day. Melton gained more than 800 yards and scored eight touchdowns as a running back in his final season at Grapevine and made Texas coaches promise he'd get a look at running back first.

"We may have another 'Bus' on our hands," says Texas coach Mack Brown. "So we'll look at Henry at running back first."

In-Vince-ible

by Chip Brown

Donald Miralle/Getty Images

Texas quarterback Vince Young didn't just break tackle after tackle in the Longhorns' 38–37 Rose Bowl victory over Michigan. Young broke out nationally as one of college football's brightest stars.

By the time Young looked back over his trail of flailing maize and blue defenders, he had four touchdowns rushing, one passing and one big, shining, silver MVP trophy in his hands.

"I've never seen a quarterback take over like that," Texas coach Mack Brown said after the game. "Vince grew up right in front of our eyes."

Because of Young's dominating performances over the final six games of last season, when he completed 63 percent of his passes and rushed for 748 yards, including 192 in the Rose Bowl, he is now being mentioned in the same sentence as the 2005 Heisman Trophy.

After two seasons of college football, Young's numbers are comparable to those of Michael Vick after Vick's only two seasons at Virginia Tech. Young has a better completion percentage (.590) than Vick did (.565) with almost the same passing yards (3,004) as Vick (3,074).

Young has more rushing yards (2,077 on a 6.8-yard average) than Vick did (1,202, 5.7) and considerably more rushing touchdowns (25) than Vick (16). The biggest difference between the two is Vick's superior touchdown-to-interception ratio — the former Hokie All-American tossed 20 TDs with only 11 interceptions, while Young has 18 TDs and 18 INTs.

Vick also led the nation in pass efficiency as a freshman while taking Virginia Tech to the national title game against Florida State.

Young, however, is developing that same reputation as a winner. He is 17–2 as a starter, and he led a 28-point comeback, the largest in school history, in a victory over Oklahoma State last season. He rushed for 22 yards on fourth-and-18 before throwing a 21-yard touchdown pass with 11 seconds left on the final drive to beat Kansas, 27–23.

And Young led a 10-play, 47-yard drive that set up UT's game-winning field goal over Michigan as time expired in the Rose Bowl.

Brown once shied away from putting unneeded pressure on Young. Now, the veteran coach says comparisons between Young and Vick are justified.

"I think it's OK because Vince is that type of player," Brown says. "And Vince has so much confidence now and is throwing the ball with such confidence and velocity. He's developing into one of the best quarterbacks in school history.

"I think comparisons to Michael Vick put pressure on Vince. But I think that's a healthy thing right now."

Talk of Young as one of college football's elite players doesn't surprise Young's mentor, Steve McNair, quarterback of the Tennessee Titans.

McNair took Young under his wing six years ago when they were introduced by Vince's uncle, Ivory Young, who played basketball at Alcorn State while McNair was setting records on the Braves' football team.

"Vince reminds me a lot of myself," McNair says. "We both grew up without father figures in our lives. I have, to some degree, tried to provide some of that fatherly advice to him and be there for him in that way.

"We both had great careers as high school quarterbacks but had schools recruit us as defensive players. That is tough to go through, knowing that you want to be and can be a college quarterback and have people tell you that you can't do it."

Young started attending McNair's football camp in Mississippi the summer after Young's sophomore year at Madison High School in Houston. Now, he serves as an instructor. Young and McNair usually talk once a week during the season.

"He helps me with everything — football, life, how to be a man," says Young, who has McNair's picture on his locker. "One of the first things Steve told me was how little kids will look up to me and to be a role model for them."

Young's high school coach at Madison, Ray Seals, was so convinced Young would become a star, he made Young take speech and drama classes to shake his habit of mumbling.

"He said, 'Coach, I don't want to take those classes,'" Seals says. "But I knew he was going to be in front of the cameras one day, and I wanted him to be able to say more than ya ya and da da."

Seals had good reason to think Young would succeed. At 6'5" and 225 pounds as a senior, Young put up ridiculous statistics. He completed 131-of-224 passes (58 percent) for 2,545 yards and 35 touchdowns with only four interceptions.

He also served as Madison's punter during his final two seasons, and he scored four touchdowns on fakes and made countless other first downs. Seals marvels most at a single sequence from Young's senior year. Young threw an interception, made the tackle, causing a fumble, recovered it, and threw a 36-yard touchdown pass on the next play.

Seals and Young's uncle, Keith Young, a quarterback in high school and college before a shoulder injury, convinced the rebellious Young that he could be a special athlete — mostly because of his size (Young was 5'5" when he was 10).

"I had to carry his birth certificate around with me when he played little league football," says Keith Young, a teacher and coach at Paul Revere Middle School in Houston. "I'd hear parents on the other team say, 'There's no way Vince Young is 10. He must be 13.'"

With success came responsibility. Young was a bully in middle school. Family members told him to use his physical gifts to help lead others, not pick on them. Now, Young takes pride in talking to young kids about doing the right thing after growing up in a home in which his mother, Felicia, was repeatedly in and out of separation with Young's father.

> "I think comparisons to Michael Vick put pressure on Vince. But I think that's a healthy thing right now."

"My mom played a big part," Young says. "She was like my mother and my father. She always stood by me. In middle school, I was going through some things, just living on the wrong road.

"My mom said, 'If you keep that up, you're going to end up dead.' It changed my whole life. I started concentrating on football and saw I could

Donald Miralle/Getty Images

be good at it and be a leader."

Madison went 10–2 Young's sophomore year, 11–2 his junior year and 14–1 his senior year, losing in the semifinals of the Class 5A state playoffs.

"People thought we had a great team," Seals says. "But Vincent took a bunch of average players and made them overachievers. They would fall behind in games and believed Vincent would get them out of it. They wanted to make plays for him."

Young narrowed a list of 50 colleges to five — Texas, Arkansas, LSU, Florida State and Southern Mississippi. But on his recruiting trip to Austin, Young was blown away and canceled the rest of his trips.

Texas offensive coordinator Greg Davis says he was stunned by Young's maturity during his in-home visit. Young asked Davis what his plans were for him. Davis said his plans were to redshirt Young.

"And then I waited for his reaction, because we pride ourselves on being up front with kids," Davis says. "And he said, 'Good. I need to redshirt. I need to learn the system. And you're one of the few who told me that that's the plan.' I immediately fell in love with the kid."

> "Vincent took a bunch of average players and made them overachievers. They would fall behind in games and believed Vincent would get them out of it. They wanted to make plays for him."

Because Young is so talented running the ball, his ability in the passing game probably doesn't get enough credit. But Young has the best completion percentage (.590) of any Texas quarterback after two seasons as a starter.

The knock on Young during his first season and a half playing at Texas was that he allowed mistakes to lead to more mistakes. He would get down on himself and press. He could also be careless with the ball when he ran.

Young's throwing motion has also been heavily scrutinized because his delivery fluctuates between three-quarters and sidearm. Errant throws, especially early in games, had some fans wondering if Young should be moved to receiver because they were convinced he couldn't play quarterback in the NFL.

"People throw it all kinds of ways," Young says. "As long as the ball gets to the receiver, that's all that matters."

What became clear as last season progressed was that Young could complete passes when the most was at stake. After throwing two interceptions and falling behind 35–7 against Oklahoma State last year, Young set the school record for completion percentage in a single game. He completed 18-of-21 (85.7 percent) for 278 yards and a touchdown as UT roared back for a 56–35 victory.

Like Chris Simms, Young has to shed the stigma of struggling against Texas' nemesis Oklahoma. Young had a fumble at the goal line and two interceptions against the Sooners in a 65–13 loss in 2003. He had two critical fumbles against OU in a 12–0 loss last season, including one deep in Sooners' territory.

Simms, however, had his meltdowns in losses to OU as a junior in 2001 (four interceptions) and as a senior in 2002 (three interceptions and four sacks). Young, who takes pride in being a gamer, will be a junior this season with what should be his best years of college football still ahead of him.

"I'm ready to just play my game," Young says. "All the other stuff takes care of itself. But I have no doubts about my abilities and what I'm capable of."

AP Wide World

2005 SEASON

Texas' 2005 season was breathtaking in its dominance.
Game by game, we relive this season for the ages.

TAKING CARE OF BUSINESS

Texas 60, Louisiana-Lafayette 3 • Game 1, Sept. 3, 2005

AUSTIN, Texas — The second-ranked Texas Longhorns barely broke a sweat, but they clearly were trying to send a message with a 60–3 romp over Louisiana-Lafayette in the season opener at Royal-Memorial Stadium.

"We went out there and took care of business," Texas junior quarterback Vince Young said. "This sent a message to whoever was watching."

The Longhorns' target audience was Columbus, Ohio, where they'll travel next for a marquee non-conference matchup with No. 6 Ohio State.

Young, who entered the season as one of the top contenders for the Heisman Trophy, showed off his arm by completing 13-of-15 passes for 173 yards and three touchdowns in the first half as Texas built a 39-3 lead. He completed passes to seven different receivers, including a pair of touchdowns to tight end Davis Thomas. Jamaal Charles set a UT freshman-debut record with 135 rushing yards.

The Longhorns went 11–1 last season with a punishing ground game behind Young and Cedric Benson, the fifth-leading career rusher in Division I-A history. Against the Ragin' Cajuns, Benson wasn't missed; the Longhorns showed off a stable of speedy and powerful running backs who helped Texas pile up 418 of its 591 yards on the ground.

The Longhorns scored on nine of their first 11 possessions and did not punt until midway through the fourth quarter.

"I thought it was very important that we showed we can run the ball," Taylor said. "Cedric was a big part of our offense last year."

The 57-point loss capped an especially difficult week for the Ragin' Cajuns, who were the only team from Louisiana to play in the wake of Hurricane Katrina. The ULL roster had 20 players from the New Orleans area.

Along with returnee Selvin Young, the new-look Texas backfield includes a pair of freshmen (Charles and 270-pounder Henry Melton) and sophomore dual-threat Ramonce Taylor. Melton broke five tackles on a 14-yard touchdown run in the third quarter and six tackles on a 22-yard score in the fourth.

"They're freshmen, but they're unusual freshmen," Texas offensive coordinator Greg Davis said of Charles and Melton.

On defense, the Longhorns allowed only a 47-yard field goal by Sean Comiskey and did not allow the Ragin' Cajuns to get closer than the 30-yard line the entire game.

"I felt like this was the perfect opener for us," Texas coach Mack Brown said.

It didn't take long for the focus to shift to the top-10 showdown with the Buckeyes at Ohio Stadium. Ohio State delivered the first blow of the week; linebacker Bobby Carpenter declared that the goal is that Young "won't be a candidate for the Heisman" after the game.

"I don't feed into all that," Young said. "Let them talk." ∎

Sporting retro helmets, Ramonce Taylor and the rest of the Longhorns laid an old-fashioned whipping on the Ragin' Cajuns.

AP Wide World

AP Wide World

Selvin Young scooted for 67 yards and a score against Louisiana-Lafayette.

Texas vs. Louisiana-Lafayette

Score by Quarters	1	2	3	4	Score	
Louisiana-Lafayette	3	0	0	0	3	Record: (0–1)
Texas	13	26	14	7	60	Record: (1–0)

Scoring Summary:

1st 08:36 UT Young, Selvin 9 yd run (McGee, Richmond kick failed), 6-35 1:44, UL 0 - UT 6
   05:32 UL Comiskey, Sean 47 yd field goal, 7-39 3:04, UL 3 - UT 6
   03:08 UT Charles, Jamaal 14 yd run (McGee, Richmond kick), 7-65 2:24, UL 3 - UT 13

2nd 13:42 UT Jones, Nate 10 yd pass from Young, Vince (McGee, Richmond kick blocked), 8-56 3:17, UL 3 - UT 19
   07:38 UT Taylor, Ramonce 30 yd run (McGee, Richmond kick blocked), 4-91 2:24, UL 3 - UT 25
   06:20 UT Thomas, David 20 yd pass from Young, Vince (McGee, Richmond kick), 1-20 0:06, UL 3 - UT 32
   00:38 UT Thomas, David 7 yd pass from Young, Vince (McGee, Richmond kick), 7-60 2:40, UL 3 - UT 39

3rd 08:21 UT Young, Vince 2 yd run (McGee, Richmond kick), 4-10 1:19, UL 3 - UT 46
   04:35 UT Melton, Henry 14 yd run (Pino, David kick), 6-34 2:11, UL 3 - UT 53

4th 14:13 UT Melton, Henry 22 yd run (Pino, David kick), 5-77 1:25, UL 3 - UT 60

	UL	UT
FIRST DOWNS	11	30
RUSHES-YARDS (NET)	34-72	52-418
PASSING YDS (NET)	166	173
Passes Att-Comp-Int	33-16-1	17-13-1
TOTAL OFFENSE PLAYS-YARDS	67-238	69-591
Fumble Returns-Yards	0-0	0-0
Punt Returns-Yards	0-0	5-106
Kickoff Returns-Yards	5-91	1-34
Interception Returns-Yards	1-11	1-4
Punts (Number-Avg)	10-40.1	2-46.0
Fumbles-Lost	2-0	4-1
Penalties-Yards	10-83	7-55
Possession Time	31:19	28:41
Third-Down Conversions	5 of 18	6 of 10
Fourth-Down Conversions	1 of 2	1 of 1
Red-Zone Scores-Chances	0-0	7-7
Sacks By: Number-Yards	0-0	3-22

RUSHING: Louisiana-Lafayette—Rubin, Caleb 9-34; Fenroy, Tyrell 7-25; Levier, Abdule 4-13; Desormeaux, Michael 7-4; Lindon, Dwight 1-1; Johnson, Chester 2-1; Jenkins, Booker 1-minus 1; Babb, Jerry 3-minus 5. Texas—Charles, Jamaal 14-135; Young, Selvin 8-67; Taylor, Ramonce 5-65; Melton, Henry 6-65; Young, Vince 7-49; Ogbonnaya, Chris 3-16; Ballew, Scott 3-14; Hobbs, Antwaun 2-10; McCoy, Matt 1-minus 1; Nordgren, Matt 3-minus 2.

PASSING: Louisiana-Lafayette—Babb, Jerry 9-18-0-109; Desormeaux, Michael 7-15-1-57. Texas—Young, Vince 13-17-1-173.

RECEIVING: Louisiana-Lafayette—Smith, Derrick 6-78; Fredrick, Corey 2-30; Fenroy, Tyrell 2-20; Givens, Ray 2-16; Jenkins, Booker 1-10; Chery, Jason 1-7; Lindon, Dwight 1-3; Roberson, Chancellor 1-2. Texas-Carter, Brian 3-65; Thomas, David 3-34; Taylor, Ramonce 2-23; Jones, Nate 2-16; Charles, Jamaal 1-18; Sweed, Limas 1-10; Cosby, Quan 1-7.

INTERCEPTIONS: Louisiana-Lafayette—Adams, Michael 1-11. Texas—Ross, Aaron 1-4.

FUMBLES: Louisiana-Lafayette—Fenroy, Tyrell 1-0; Babb, Jerry 1-0.
Texas—Nordgren, Matt 1-0; McCoy, Matt 1-0; Young, Selvin 1-1; Melton, Henry 1-0.

Stadium: Royal-Texas Memorial
Attendance: 82,519

HORNS MAKE HISTORY IN THE HORSESHOE

Texas 25, Ohio State 22 • Game 2, Sept. 10, 2005

COLUMBUS, Ohio – Texas heard the entire week leading up to its Showdown at the Horseshoe how they had no chance to beat Ohio State. How Vince Young's Heisman candidacy would end as quickly as you can say, "Ted Ginn Jr." and how no team outside the Big Ten had left Ohio Stadium with a victory in 15 years.

The Longhorns didn't even flinch.

Vince Young added another chapter in his growing legend – only this time he won a game with his arm, not his legs, tossing a 24-yard touchdown to Limas Sweed with 2:37 remaining to rally the No. 2 Longhorns past No. 4 Ohio State 25–22 in the first meeting between two of college football's most storied programs.

Texas snapped an eight-game losing streak against Top 10 opponents dating to a 24–20 win over No. 3 Nebraska in 1999. The win was the second straight for the Longhorns over a Big Ten powerhouse. They defeated Michigan in the Rose Bowl, when Young rushed for 192 yards and accounted for five touchdowns.

Ohio State had not lost a non-conference home game since 1990 – a span of 36 games – and was unbeaten in six previous night games at Ohio Stadium.

"All the kids that watched TV said nobody gave us any chance and you can't win here," Texas coach Mack Brown said.

To pull off one of the biggest victories in school history, the Longhorns had to survive a shaky first three quarters when they had three turnovers that wiped out a 10-point lead and watched a school record-tying five field goals by Ohio State kicker John Huston.

With the Longhorns down 22–16 with five minutes left, Young engineered a season-making six-play, 67-yard drive. He converted a critical nine-yard completion to freshman Jamaal Charles on third-and-six, only to be briefly shaken up on a one-yard scramble toward the right side a short time later that forced the Longhorns to take a timeout. Young shook off the cobwebs to find Sweed, who made a leaping backward catch in double coverage in the left corner of the end zone. It was the first collegiate touchdown reception for Sweed, quickly cementing his place in Longhorn lore. Billy Pittman, who did not have a reception in the season opener against Louisiana-Lafayette, was another Longhorn hero, posting five catches for 130 yards.

"I was walking down the sidelines telling the guys, 'We've been though this play by play,'" Young said. "The defense is going to give us the ball and they did a great job."

For the game, Young passed for 270 yards and ran for 76 more, accounting for 346 of Texas' 382 total yards.

"He was hit and beat up and kept coming back," Ohio State coach Jim Tressel said. "We have a lot of respect for him."

AP Wide World

Texas wide receiver Billy Pittman, center, celebrates his touchdown against Ohio State with Will Allen, left, and Limas Sweed.

AP Wide World

The game might have turned into a rout had the Buckeyes been able to find the end zone. Ohio State came up with three turnovers inside Texas territory, but the Buckeyes had to settle for field goals each time. Huston hit field goals of 45, 36, 25, 44 and 26 yards, but his biggest moment was a 50-yard attempt that sailed wide right with five minutes remaining and kept the score at 22–16.

Texas came up with two big plays during the game's final two minutes. Outside linebacker Drew Kelson stripped the ball loose from Buckeyes quarterback Justin Zwick, and Brian Robison recovered the fumble. Middle linebacker Aaron Harris provided the finishing touch with a sack of Troy Smith in the end zone for a safety with 19 seconds remaining.

Cornerback Cedric Griffin saved a potential touchdown with a jarring hit on tight end Ryan Hamby in the end zone in the third quarter.

Down 10–0, Ohio State began its comeback as

Vince Young and the rest of the Longhorns came of age on a warm Columbus night with one of the all-time gut-check wins. (Right) Texas linebacker Brian Robison picks up a fumble in the fourth quarter.

Smith replaced Zwick at quarterback and led the Buckeyes on five scoring drives.

Ohio State linebacker A.J. Hawk had a monster performance with two sacks, a fumble recovery and interception. But explosive playmaker Ted Ginn Jr. was contained by the UT defense and finished with two catches for nine yards and was never able to break free on kick returns.

With a three-point victory, Brown had silenced his critics who said he couldn't win the big game, the Longhorns made a legitimate case as national title contenders and Young left as a Heisman frontrunner.

All in all, not a bad night in the Horseshoe. ■

AP Wide World

AP Wide World

Young accumulated 346 yards of total offense, bouncing back from one brutal hit after another.

Texas vs. Ohio State

Score by Quarters	1	2	3	4	Score	
Texas	10	3	3	9	25	Record: (2-0)
Ohio State	0	16	6	0	22	Record: (1-1)

Scoring Summary:

1st 10:03 UT   Pino, David 42 yd field goal, 11-64 3:54, UT 3 - OHIO ST. 0
    01:37 UT   Pittman, Billy 5 yd pass from Young, Vince (Pino, David kick), 10-84 4:03, UT 10 - OHIO ST. 0

2nd 14:17 OHIO ST   Huston, Josh 45 yd field goal, 5-8 2:13, UT 10 - OHIO ST. 3
    08:11 OHIO ST.   Holmes, Santonio 36 yd pass from Smith, Troy (Huston, Josh kick), 9-80 3:25, UT 10 - OHIO ST. 10
    04:33 OHIO ST.   Huston, Josh 36 yd field goal, 4--1 1:55, UT 10 - OHIO ST. 13
    00:35 OHIO ST.   Huston, Josh 25 yd field goal, 9-22 3:14, UT 10 - OHIO ST. 16
    00:02 UT   Pino, David 37 yd field goal, 4-34 0:29, UT 13 - OHIO ST. 16

3rd 11:46 OHIO ST.   Huston, Josh 44 yd field goal, 6-11 2:33, UT 13 - OHIO ST. 19
    07:36 UT   Pino, David 25 yd field goal, 7-72 4:10, UT 16 - OHIO ST. 19
    05:12 OHIO ST.   Huston, Josh 26 yd field goal, 7-45 2:16, UT 16 - OHIO ST. 22

4th 02:37 UT   Sweed, Limas 24 yd pass from Young, Vince (Pino, David kick), 7-67 2:23, UT 23 - OHIO ST. 22
    00:19 UT   TEAM safety, , UT 25 - OHIO ST. 22

	UT	OHIO ST.
FIRST DOWNS	19	13
RUSHES-YARDS (NET)	38-112	36-111
PASSING YDS (NET)	270	144
Passes Att-Comp-Int	29-18-2	26-14-0
TOTAL OFFENSE PLAYS-YARDS	67-382	62-255
Fumble Returns-Yards	1-9	0-0
Punt Returns-Yards	1-1	1-8
Kickoff Returns-Yards	4-91	6-191
Interception Returns-Yards	0-0	2-24
Punts (Number-Avg)	4-38.0	4-39.5
Fumbles-Lost	4-1	3-1
Penalties-Yards	4-30	8-78
Possession Time	30:09	29:51
Third-Down Conversions	4 of 12	5 of 15
Fourth-Down Conversions	0 of 1	0 of 0
Red-Zone Scores-Chances	3-4	3-3
Sacks By: Number-Yards	4-20	3-15

RUSHING: Texas-Young, Vince 20-76; Charles, Jamaal 10-26; Young, Selvin 5-11; Melton, Henry 2-2; TEAM 1-minus 3. Ohio State-Pittman, Antonio 17-75; Smith, Troy 13-27; Zwick, Justin 5-11; Ginn, Jr., Ted 1-minus 2.

PASSING: Texas-Young, Vince 18-29-2-270. Ohio State-Zwick, Justin 9-15-0-66; Smith, Troy 5-11-0-78.

RECEIVING: Texas-Charles, Jamaal 6-69; Pittman, Billy 5-130; Sweed, Limas 3-46; Taylor, Ramonce 2-3; Carter, Brian 1-13; Thomas, David 1-9. Ohio State-Holmes, S 4-73; Gonzalez, Anthony 2-33; Hall, Roy 2-19; Ginn, Jr., Ted 2-9; Hamby, Ryan 2-9; Pittman, Antonio 2-1.

INTERCEPTIONS: Texas-None. Ohio State-Salley, Nate 1-0; Hawk, A.J. 1-24.

FUMBLES: Young, Vince 2-0; Young, Selvin 1-1; Charles, Jamaal 1-0. Ohio State-TEAM 1-0; Smith, Troy 1-0; Zwick, Justin 1-1.

Stadium: Ohio Stadium
Attendance: 105,565

CHARLES LEADS THE CHARGE

Texas 51, Rice 10 • Game 3, Sept. 17, 2005

AUSTIN, Texas – Texas coach Mack Brown should know something about talented running backs. He coached Heisman Trophy winner Ricky Williams in 1998 and spent the last four years with Cedric Benson.

He thinks true freshman Jamaal Charles can be a special player.

Charles, an 18-year-old from Port Arthur, Texas, rushed 16 times for 189 yards and three touchdowns to lead No. 2 Texas to a 51–10 victory over Rice before 83,055 at Royal-Memorial Stadium.

It was the second-best rushing performance by a freshman in school history behind Benson's 213 yards against Kansas in 2001. Charles, who started at tailback for injured Selvin Young, accounted for the Longhorns' first three scores with two touchdown runs of 25 yards and another of four yards.

"He is a special freshman," Texas offensive coordinator Greg Davis said. "Football comes easy to him. He's way ahead of schedule for a freshman."

In the season opener against Louisiana-Lafayette, Charles had 135 yards rushing, and he had two key receptions on the Longhorns' game-winning drive against Ohio State.

After each of his touchdown runs, Charles showed

Matt Melton and the Longhorn defense dominated the outmanned Owls.

his age by walking over to quarterback Vince Young on the sideline asking the same question.

"How'd I do?" Charles asked.

Young always told him the same thing: "Just fine."

Charles had four runs of at least 20 yards among his first 10 carries against Rice's nation-worst run defense as Texas built a 42–0 lead by halftime. He would have threatened the UT single-game rushing record by a freshman but was taken out of the

Eight tackles and a defensive touchdown: just another day at the office for Michael Huff.

Cedric who? Jamaal Charles continued his stellar play with 189 yards rushing and three scores.

game early in the third quarter.

"My goal every time is to run for 200 yards," Charles said.

Leading 21–0, Texas turned to its aggressive, hard-hitting defense in the second quarter. Strong safety Michael Huff picked up a loose ball and returned it 21 yards for a touchdown, and middle linebacker Aaron Harris jarred the ball loose on a vicious hit of Rice backup quarterback Chase Clement near the Owls' goal line. Defensive tackle Frank Okam fell on the ball in the end zone for a 35–0 lead. It was a welcome development, considering that during the two previous games, the Longhorns had forced only two turnovers.

Texas limited Rice's option attack to 110 yards on the ground and 209 total yards for the game. The Owls didn't score until Brennan Landry's 37-yard field goal late in the third quarter. Clement added a

two-yard touchdown run midway through the fourth quarter.

"We're very adamant about not having letdowns," Texas co-defensive coordinator Gene Chizik said. "If we're going to be a championship defense, you have to play one way all the time."

Vince Young followed up the electrifying win over Ohio State a week earlier by completing 8-of-14 passes for 101 yards and adding another 77 yards on eight carries. ▪

Texas vs. Rice

Score by Quarters	1	2	3	4	Score	
Rice	0	0	3	7	10	Record: (0-2)
Texas	14	28	9	0	51	Record: (3-0)

Scoring Summary:

1st 13:11 UT Charles, Jamaal 25 yd run (Pino, David kick), 6-80 1:49, RICE 0 - UT 7
07:16 UT Charles, Jamaal 25 yd run (Pino, David kick), 7-99 3:12, RICE 0 - UT 14

2nd 11:16 UT Charles, Jamaal 4 yd run (Pino, David kick), 6-68 2:38, RICE 0 - UT 21
10:07 UT Huff, Michael 21 yd fumble recovery (Pino, David kick), RICE 0 - UT 28
05:27 UT Okam, Frank 0 yd fumble recovery (Pino, David kick), RICE 0 - UT 35
01:11 UT Melton, Henry 1 yd run (Pino, David kick), 7-70 1:50, RICE 0 - UT 42

3rd 10:02 UT Pino, David 40 yd field goal, 7-40 2:10, RICE 0 - UT 45
05:49 RICE Landry 37 yd field goal, 8-39 4:13, RICE 3 - UT 45
01:34 UT Taylor, Ramonce 10 yd run (Pino, David kick failed), 4-33 1:46, RICE 3 - UT 51

4th 07:28 RICE Clement 2 yd run (Landry kick), 9-71 3:53, RICE 10 - UT 51

	RICE	UT
FIRST DOWNS	12	24
RUSHES-YARDS (NET)	46-110	47-361
PASSING YDS (NET)	99	122
Passes Att-Comp-Int	15-4-0	18-11-1
TOTAL OFFENSE PLAYS-YARDS	61-209	65-483
Fumble Returns-Yards	0-0	1-21
Punt Returns-Yards	0-0	4-15
Kickoff Returns-Yards	6-104	1-31
Interception Returns-Yards	1-0	0-0
Punts (Number-Avg)	7-44.3	4-47.0
Fumbles-Lost	3-2	2-0
Penalties-Yards	7-49	10-87
Possession Time	29:23	30:37
Third-Down Conversions	4 of 15	5 of 12
Fourth-Down Conversions	0 of 2	0 of 0
Red-Zone Scores-Chances	2-3	3-3
Sacks By: Number-Yards	1-7	2-17

RUSHING: Rice-Q.Smith 11-76; Clement 7-16; Wall 4-14; Rucker 4-11; Cates 4-8; Henderson 2-1; Bilaye-Benibo 4-1; Rice Team 1-minus 3; Dillard 1-minus 7; Armstrong 8-minus 7. Texas-Charles, Jamaal 16-189; Young, Vince 8-77; Melton, Henry 14-75; Taylor, Ramonce 2-14; Ogbonnaya, Chris 3-6; Nordgren, Matt 2-4; Ballew, Scott 1-0; McCoy, Matt 1-minus 4.

PASSING: Rice-Clement 2-8-0-57; Armstrong 2-7-0-42. Texas-Young, Vince 8-14-1-101; Nordgren, Matt 3-4-0-21.

RECEIVING: Rice-Dillard 2-70; Aranda 2-29. Texas-Thomas, David 5-66; Jones, Nate 2-17; Sweed, Limas 1-21; Cosby, Quan 1-7; Charles, Jamaal 1-7; Gatewood, Tyrell 1-4.

INTERCEPTIONS: Rice-JaC.Shepherd 1-0. Texas-None.

FUMBLES: Rice-Clement 1-1; Q.Smith 1-1; Rice Team 1-0. Texas-Charles, Jamaal 1-0; McCoy, Matt 1-0.

Stadium: Royal-Texas Memorial
Attendance: 83,055

NO LOOKING AHEAD

Texas 51, Missouri 20 • Game 4, Oct. 1, 2005

COLUMBIA, Mo. – Texas coach Mack Brown warned his players about looking ahead to facing Oklahoma the following week. For awhile it looked like the second-ranked Longhorns weren't listening, as they committed enough mistakes to allow Missouri to hang around for a quarter.

The Longhorns had 14 penalties for 135 yards, four fumbles, three dropped snaps and a missed extra point – yet Texas still managed to win in a blowout, 51–20 in its Big 12 Conference opener at Faurot Field.

"We've got a chance to be really good, and we haven't played near our best game yet," Brown said. "The fun thing is we're 4–0, and we haven't scratched the surface."

In a tune-up for its annual grudge match with OU, the Longhorns repeatedly made Missouri pay for its mistakes. Vince Young ran for 108 yards and a touchdown and threw for two other scores, and Texas converted three first-half turnovers by quarterback Brad Smith into quick touchdowns.

"Our bunch can score fast," Brown said. "That's what we've got to continue to do. We should have scored a lot more today."

The Longhorns led 14–13 after one quarter and then ran off 37 straight points before Smith scored again with 3:54 left.

Missouri, which entered the game fifth in the nation in total offense at 554 yards per game, could not keep up with the Texas offense and was held to 330 yards. Smith, one of the country's most explosive dual-threat quarterbacks, had two touchdown runs for the Tigers but was harassed throughout the game and sacked four times. He completed only 19-of-37 passes for 181 yards and accounted for all three of Missouri's turnovers – two fumbles and an interception.

The Longhorns accumulated 585 yards of total offense and reached the 50-point plateau for the third time in four games. It could have been worse, with true freshman Jamaal Charles fumbling the ball out of the end zone in the third quarter and a second-quarter drive that stalled at the Missouri 4-yard line.

The Longhorns had three one-play scoring drives in the first half – all of them resulting from turnovers by Smith – that took only 42 seconds off the clock.

"They're a good team, I ain't going to lie," Missouri safety David Overstreet said. "At first, I had my doubts that they were a legit No. 2, but after today I know they really deserve to be the No. 2 team in the nation."

Young, who injured his right index finger in the first half, completed 15-of-22 passes for 236 yards. He finished with 108 yards for his eighth career 100-yard rushing performance and first of the season. Young gave the Longhorns some breathing room just before halftime, when he scrambled 34

Ramonce Taylor caught a 27-yard TD pass from Vince Young.

yards on third-and-30 to set up a 26-yard field goal by David Pino to make it 24–13.

"I told the guys in the huddle I need time in the pocket to make three or four sand-wiches," Young joked.

Charles finished with 15 carries for 97 yards and two touch-downs, giving him five scores in the last two games.

The decisive stretch for the Tigers came in the first quarter when Smith was intercepted by Texas linebacker Aaron Harris on the third play of the game, setting up Charles' 3-yard run. Smith fumbled on a sack later in the quarter, and Young went untouched on a 33-yard draw on the next play to put Texas ahead 14–7.

Smith's second fumble gave Texas the ball at the Missouri 22 early in the second quarter. After a holding call, Charles caught a 32-yard touch-down pass for a touchdown.

"We don't feel like anybody can stop us," UT tailback Selvin Young said. "I guess the biggest fear is that we stop ourselves."

The Longhorns opened the second half with a six-play, 80-yard drive capped by Ramonce Taylor's one-handed grab of a swing pass and acrobatic dive into the end zone that made the score 31–13.

"I saw the safety coming down and he had the angle on me, so I just tried to beat him to the end zone," Taylor said. "I've got a feeling it will

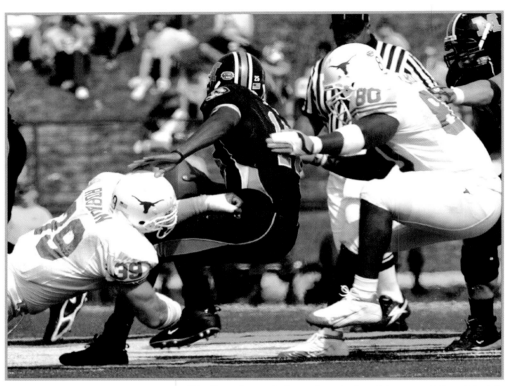

The Longhorn defense harried and harassed Brad Smith and the Missouri offense into three turnovers.

be on SportsCenter."

Henry Melton added a pair of one-yard runs in the second half, and Aaron Ross returned a punt 88 yards for a touchdown, the third-longest punt return in program history.

"We could have probably scored 70-something points," offensive tackle Jonathan Scott said.

Texas players said they heard plenty of trash talk through the first half from Missouri players. A year earlier, the Tigers played the Longhorns much closer in a 28–20 loss in Austin.

So, to prove a point, center Lyle Sendlein told the Tigers exactly where UT was going to run the ball on one play.

The Longhorns scored on the play.

It's been that kind of season for the Longhorns, who can seemingly do little wrong. ■

Texas vs. Missouri

Score by Quarters	1	2	3	4	Score	
Texas	14	10	13	14	51	Record: (4-0,1-0)
Missouri	13	0	0	7	20	Record: (2-2,0-1)

Scoring Summary:

1st 13:47 UT Charles, Jamaal 3 yd run (Pino, David kick), 1-3 0:03, UT 7 - MU 0
10:06 MU Jackson, Jimmy 12 yd run (Crossett, Adam kick), 11-87 3:41, UT 7 - MU 7
06:29 UT Young, Vince 33 yd run (Pino, David kick), 1-33 0:07, UT 14 - MU 7
01:13 MU Smith, Brad 3 yd run (Crossett, Adam kick failed), 13-80 5:16, UT 14 - MU 13

2nd 10:06 UT Charles, Jamaal 32 yd pass from Young, Vince (Pino, David kick), 1-22 0:32, UT 21 - MU 13
03:22 UT Pino, David 26 yd field goal, 14-52 4:44, UT 24 - MU 13

3rd 13:50 UT Taylor, Ramonce 27 yd pass from Young, Vince (Pino, David kick), 6-80 1:10, UT 31 - MU 13
08:46 UT Melton, Henry 1 yd run (Pino, David kick failed), 7-40 2:34, UT 37 - MU 13

4th 10:18 UT Melton, Henry 1 yd run (Pino, David kick), 9-55 4:42, UT 44 - MU 13
08:02 UT Ross, Aaron 88 yd punt return (Pino, David kick), UT 51 - MU 13
03:54 MU Smith, Brad 1 yd run (Crossett, Adam kick), 11-72 4:08, UT 51 - MU 20

	UT	MU
FIRST DOWNS	23	27
RUSHES-YARDS (NET)	50-349	47-139
PASSING YDS (NET)	236	191
Passes Att-Comp-Int	22-15-1	39-21-1
TOTAL OFFENSE PLAYS-YARDS	72-585	86-330
Fumble Returns-Yards	0-0	0-0
Punt Returns-Yards	4-129	0-0
Kickoff Returns-Yards	3-74	7-120
Interception Returns-Yards	1-30	1-0
Punts (Number-Avg)	2-36.5	7-42.0
Fumbles-Lost	4-1	4-2
Penalties-Yards	14-135	5-31
Possession Time	29:30	30:30
Third-Down Conversions	5 of 10	8 of 18
Fourth-Down Conversions	1 of 2	1 of 2
Red-Zone Scores-Chances	4-7	3-3
Sacks By: Number-Yards	4-29	1-13

RUSHING: Texas-Young, Vince 13-108; Charles, Jamaal 15-97; Young, Selvin 11-65; Melton, Henry 9-57; Pittman, Billy 1-19; Myers, Marcus 1-3. Missouri-Smith, Brad 25-57; Woods, Marcus 12-46; Jackson, Jimmy 5-36; Franklin, Willi 2-10; Saunders, Tommy 1-6; Daniel, Chase 1-minus 2; TEAM 1-minus 14.

PASSING: Texas-Young, Vince 15-22-1-236. Missouri-Smith, Brad 19-37-1-181; Daniel, Chase 2-2-0-10.

RECEIVING: Texas-Pittman, Billy 4-81; Taylor, Ramonce 3-55; Carter, Brian 3-31; Charles, Jamaal 2-30; Thomas, David 2-26; Sweed, Limas 1-13. Missouri-Coffey, Sean 6-43; Rucker, Martin 5-57; Coffman, Chase 3-39; Jackson, Jimmy 3-12; Ekwerekwu, Brad 1-20; Britt, Arnold 1-13; Woods, Marcus 1-4; Smith, Brad 1-3.

INTERCEPTIONS: Texas-Harris, Aaron 1-30. Missouri-Bacon, Marcus 1-0.

FUMBLES: Texas-Young, Vince 2-0; Charles, Jamaal 1-1. Missouri-Smith, Brad 3-2; Johnson, Domono 1-0.

Stadium: Faurot Field
Attendance: 57,231

OVER THE HUMP

Texas 45, Oklahoma 12 • Game 5, Oct. 8, 2005

DALLAS, Texas – No matter what great things are in store for the Texas Longhorns the remainder of the 2005 season, nothing would have really mattered had they not figured out a way to beat nemesis Oklahoma.

Coming off five consecutive losses – including a few embarrassing blowouts – at the hands of the Sooners, Texas got over the hump and whipped Oklahoma 45–12 in the Red River Rivalry at the Cotton Bowl.

"One of the things I have noticed after the last few years is the respect for these two teams for each other," Texas coach Mack Brown said. "The Sooners have both won so many games and they know when they play each other it's usually two of the top ten football teams in the country."

The Longhorns, who improved to 5–0, looked on this day every bit as good as their national ranking of second by snapping their longest losing streak in the 100-game series since the 1950s.

"In the locker room, you could tell everyone was really excited and ready to play," Texas defensive tackle Rod Wright said. "We had the attitude to go out there and play our best game."

After the game, quarterback Vince Young led a burnt orange victory parade in front of the stands and slapped high-fives with Longhorn supporters who had suffered so much heartbreak in Dallas in recent years.

"We wanted them to feel everything we were feeling," Young said.

The victory was a huge hurdle for the Longhorns on their path to the school's first outright national championship since 1969. They've won 12 games in a row since last year's 12–0 loss to the Sooners.

"We've had a tough time in this series. I'm not proud of that and I feel responsible for that," Brown said. "To see the kids out on the field with the fans, the interaction after the game, is something you really feel good about."

Oklahoma didn't have a play cover more than nine yards until there was 12:04 left in the game and they were down 38–6. The 33-point margin of victory matched the largest in the series for the Longhorns, who won 40–7 in 1941.

"They are an excellent football team, which we knew coming in, and they showed it again today," said Sooners coach Bob Stoops, whose team had beaten the Longhorns by a combined score of 189–54 the previous five years.

Texas rolled up 444 yards of total offense, while holding the Sooners to just 171 yards. Young passed for 241 yards and ran for 45 yards, and freshman tailback Jamaal Charles added 116 yards rushing on only nine carries.

"I took it upon myself this week to know my protective schemes," Young said. "Oklahoma throws a lot at you. So I made it a point to get my head ready and the mental part of the game ready so that I would be prepared this year."

The Longhorns took the opening kickoff and

Jamaal Charles' 80-yard run unleashed a long-awaited Red River rout for the Longhorns.

Billy Pittman (above) and Ramonce Taylor (facing page) made life miserable for the OU secondary, combining for 137 yards receiving and three touchdowns.

drove 82 yards in 12 plays, taking a 7–0 lead on Young's 15-yard touchdown pass to Ramonce Taylor. Young was 5-for-5 for 60 yards on the drive to give Texas its first lead over the Sooners in three years.

The Sooners answered with a pair of field goals to get within 7–6, but Charles ripped off an 80-yard touchdown run to give Texas a 14–6 lead at the end of the first quarter.

In the second quarter, Texas benefited from a pass interference penalty against Oklahoma linebacker Zach Latimer that wiped out an interception thrown by Young. The Longhorns ended up with a field goal on the drive and added a backbreaking touchdown just before halftime when Young found Billy Pittman alone for a 64-yard pass with 17 seconds left.

"I thought that play in the second quarter (the Oklahoma interception that was called back) was really a breaking point for us," Stoops said. "That was a big swing."

Texas led 24–6 at the half and put the game out of reach late in the third quarter when Young threw a 27-yard touchdown pass to Pittman, who made a one-handed catch to make the score 31–6.

The Sooners were hampered with running back Adrian Peterson on the sideline for most of the game with a right ankle sprain suffered the previous week against Kansas State. Peterson, who rushed for 225 yards against Texas last year and was the runner-up for the Heisman Trophy, was limited to

Run, big fella! Rodrique Wright punctuated a day of dominance with a 67-yard TD rumble with an OU fumble.

three early rushing attempts for 10 yards.

"We wanted to give them some different looks," UT co-defensive coordinator Gene Chizik said. "I think it unfolded close to what we had hoped for. We wanted to stop the running game and put the quarterback in situations where the whole stadium knew he had to throw."

The Longhorns come out of the Oklahoma game undefeated for the first time since 1983, when they won their first 11 games before losing to Georgia in the Cotton Bowl in a game that cost them a national championship.

"I'm excited about where we are and where I think we're going," Brown said. "I don't think we've played near out best game. We're 5–0 but we have improvement to make in many areas. We have a chance to be special." ■

Texas vs. Oklahoma

Score by Quarters	1	2	3	4	Score	
Oklahoma	6	0	0	6	12	Record: (2-3,1-1)
Texas	14	10	7	14	45	Record: (5-0,2-0)

Scoring Summary:

1st 09:04 UT Taylor, Ramonce 15 yd pass from Young, Vince (Pino, David kick), 12-82 5:56, OU 0 - UT 7
04:16 OU Hartley, Garrett 52 yd field goal, 6-13 1:50, OU 3 - UT 7
01:31 OU Hartley, Garrett 26 yd field goal, 6-17 2:40, OU 6 - UT 7
01:18 UT Charles, Jamaal 80 yd run (Pino, David kick), 1-80 0:13, OU 6 - UT 14

2nd 03:46 UT Pino, David 37 yd field goal, 8-32 3:08, OU 6 - UT 17
00:17 UT Pittman, Billy 64 yd pass from Young, Vince (Pino, David kick), 2-70 0:38, OU 6 - UT 24

3rd 05:26 UT Pittman, Billy 27 yd pass from Young, Vince (Pino, David kick), 6-53 2:28, OU 6 - UT 31
4th 13:06 UT Young, Selvin 5 yd run (Pino, David kick), 10-64 3:34, OU 6 - UT 38

11:35 OU Finley, Joe Jon 15 yd pass from Bomar, Rhett (Bomar, Rhett pass failed), 5-38 1:22, OU 12 - UT 38
s07:41 UT Wright, Rodrique 67 yd fumble recovery (Pino, David kick), , OU 12 - UT 45

	OU	UT
FIRST DOWNS	12	20
RUSHES-YARDS (NET)	33-77	40-203
PASSING YDS (NET)	94	241
Passes Att-Comp-Int	33-12-1	27-14-0
TOTAL OFFENSE PLAYS-YARDS	66-171	67-444
Fumble Returns-Yards	0-0	1-67
Punt Returns-Yards	1-5	2-6
Kickoff Returns-Yards	8-126	1-18
Interception Returns-Yards	0-0	1-0
Punts (Number-Avg)	7-39.9	5-37.0
Fumbles-Lost	1-1	3-1
Penalties-Yards	6-50	12-110
Possession Time	29:41	30:19
Third-Down Conversions	6 of 18	6 of 15
Fourth-Down Conversions	1 of 1	2 of 2
Red-Zone Scores-Chances	2-3	3-3
Sacks By: Number-Yards	3-14	3-21

RUSHING: Oklahoma-Hickson, Donta 5-22; Jones, Kejuan 8-19; Gutierrez, Jacob 3-15; Peterson, Adrian 3-10; Bomar, Rhett 12-9; Runnels, J.D. 1-3; TEAM 1-minus 1. Texas-Charles, Jamaal 9-116; Young, Vince 17-45; Young, Selvin 11-45; Melton, Henry 2-0; TEAM 1-minus 3.

PASSING: Oklahoma-Bomar, Rhett 12-33-1-94. Texas-Young, Vince 14-27-0-241.

RECEIVING: Oklahoma-Finley, Joe John 2-21; Jones, Kejuan 2-17; Gutierrez, Jacob 2-7; Rankins, Jejuan 1-17; Iglesias, Juaquin 1-9; Wilson, Travis 1-8; Runnels, J.D. 1-6; Thompson, Paul 1-6; Johnson, Manuel 1-3. Texas-Thomas, David 5-50; Pittman, Billy 4-100; Taylor, Ramonce 2-37; Sweed, Limas 2-32; Carter, Brian 1-22.

INTERCEPTIONS: Oklahoma-None. Texas-Huff, Michael 1-0.

FUMBLES: Oklahoma-Bomar, Rhett 1-1. Texas-Young, Vince 1-0; Brown, Tarell 1-0; Young, Selvin 1-1.

Stadium: Cotton Bowl
Attendance: 75,452

ANOTHER LONGHORN STAMPEDE

Texas 42, Colorado 17 • Game 6, Oct. 15, 2005

AUSTIN, Texas – Texas quarterback Vince Young wasn't about to allow his team to suffer a letdown.

With the Longhorns coming off an emotional victory over Oklahoma that snapped a five-game losing streak to the Sooners, Young was nearly perfect in leading second-ranked Texas to a 42–17 wipeout of No. 24 Colorado at Royal-Memorial Stadium.

Behind a dominating performance from the offensive line, Young threw for a career-high 336 yards and ran for three first-half touchdowns to lead the Longhorns to their seventh consecutive win over a ranked team.

"I think Colorado is a really good football team, but Vince's performance was the best today that I have ever seen him," Texas coach Mack Brown said. "He just made play after play."

The win was the 13th in a row for the Longhorns, who improved to 6–0 heading into an important game next week against undefeated Texas Tech.

"I do think we're one of the best teams in the nation," Brown said. "I don't think there is any doubt about that right now, but I want to see us continue. Next week we are playing another undefeated team."

In a possible preview of the Big 12 championship game, the nation's second-ranked rushing offense (288.6) went to the air with three receivers hauling in at least five receptions and seven catching at least one. Limas Sweed led the Longhorns with seven catches, two of them for touchdowns covering 35 and 13 yards.

Colorado came into the game allowing only 77.6 rushing yards per game, sixth-best in the country. Texas also played all but one first-quarter possession without leading rusher Jamaal Charles, who was bothered by a sprained left ankle.

It didn't matter. That simply gave the Longhorn passing attack an opportunity to shine.

Texas rolled up 482 yards of offense while holding Colorado to 237 yards. The Longhorns led 28–0 midway through the second quarter on touchdown runs of one, 16 and nine yards by Young and a five-yard run by Selvin Young.

"Everybody was open because they put so many people on the line of scrimmage and we didn't want to be stubborn," Brown said. "We rushed for 147 yards or something and that's okay. For Vince to have that many throws that open, I think it's great for us to be the second-leading rushing team in the nation and throw over 336 yards with Vince.

"That tells people we have the ability to do both. The question coming out of the Rose Bowl (last year) was if Vince and the receiving corps were ready to have a passing attack, and I think we answered that."

Young completed 25-of-29 passes, setting a school record with an 86.2 completion rate. He was 16-of-18 in the first half for 258 yards as the Longhorns scored on all five first-half possessions for a 35–10

This day was vintage Vince Young: 336 yards passing and two TDs, 58 yards rushing and two more scores.

halftime lead.

"The biggest thing for this game was using what the coaches taught me all week and making sure I get all the guys involved," Young said. "I am trying to get better each week."

The Longhorns went 90 yards in 16 plays on their first possession of the game, taking a 7–0 lead on Young's one-yard plunge. Texas converted three first downs on the drive and a fourth-and-four at the Colorado 40 when Young hit Brian Carter for 24 yards.

Young's winding 16-yard run late in the first quarter made it 14–0, capping a 67-yard drive.

"I think they know that he is a true leader and a great competitor and they understand how tough Vince is," Brown said. "Your quarterback is your leader, whether he wants to be or not, and Vince does love it. He likes that role of leading the football team. He came up to me after I jumped the guys on Tuesday and said, 'Hey coach you're fine, don't worry about it.' And he played that way."

Following a Texas interception of Colorado quarterback Joel Klatt, Young connected with Billy Pittman for 62 yards to set up Selvin Young's five-yard touchdown run that made it 21–0.

Vince Young capped the first half scoring for the Longhorns with a nine-yard run and a delicate 35-yard pass to Sweed in the end zone that put Texas ahead 35–3.

"I thought (Vince Young) stayed focused," Brown said. "It's easy when you score that easily to lose focus sometimes. I thought he made really good deci-

Young stretches for the pylon on one of the greatest days of his brilliant career.

sions because there was twice when he hit the deep post to Billy Pittman that I screamed to run and I'm glad he didn't hear me.

"When he hit Limas for the touchdown, I screamed 'Selvin is open,' and I hoped nobody heard me. He is making great decisions right now and it is fun to watch him play. I thought it was an unbelievable play when he was sprinting towards our bench and then threw back to Billy.

"It just breaks teams' backs, and those are things that he couldn't do at midseason last year. He is a fun player to watch right now and our guys are feeding off of him. I thought this was as good as he looked since that second half against Oklahoma State." ■

Texas vs. Colorado

Score by Quarters	1	2	3	4	Score	
Colorado	0	10	0	7	17	Record: (4-2, 2-1)
Texas	14	21	0	7	42	Record: (6-0, 3-0)

Scoring Summary:

1st 05:46 UT Young, Vince 1 yd run (Pino, David kick), 16-90 7:40, CU 0 - UT 7
　　00:52 UT Young, Vince 16 yd run (Pino, David kick), 6-67 3:05, CU 0 - UT 14

2nd 10:27 UT Young, Selvin 5 yd run (Pino, David kick), 4-75 1:52, CU 0 - UT 21
　　06:04 UT Young, Vince 9 yd run (Pino, David kick), 8-37 3:14, CU 0 - UT 28
　　03:10 CU Crosby, Mason 48 yd field goal, 11-47 2:54, CU 3 - UT 28
　　01:39 UT Sweed, Limas 35 yd pass from Young, Vince (Pino, David kick), 5-72 1:31, CU 3 - UT 35
　　00:01 CU Judge, Evan 8 yd pass from Klatt, Joel (Crosby, Mason kick), 8-64 1:38, CU 10 - UT 35

4th 14:06 UT Sweed, Limas 13 yd pass from Young, Vince (Pino, David kick), 9-49 4:10, CU 10 - UT 42
　　09:40 CU Klopfenstein, Joe 4 yd pass from Klatt, Joel (Crosby, Mason kick), 4-5 0:52, CU 17 - UT 42

	CU	UT
FIRST DOWNS	14	24
RUSHES-YARDS (NET)	19-45	47-145
PASSING YDS (NET)	192	337
Passes Att-Comp-Int	44-21-1	32-26-0
TOTAL OFFENSE PLAYS-YARDS	63-237	79-482
Fumble Returns-Yards	0-0	0-0
Punt Returns-Yards	2-6	4-24
Kickoff Returns-Yards	5-89	2-51
Interception Returns-Yards	0-0	1-5
Punts (Number-Avg)	7-40.1	3-39.7
Fumbles-Lost	2-1	2-1
Penalties-Yards	11-83	8-70
Possession Time	21:06	38:54
Third-Down Conversions	6 of 15	10 of 17
Fourth-Down Conversions	1 of 1	2 of 2
Red-Zone Scores-Chances	2-2	5-7
Sacks By: Number-Yards	0-0	0-0

RUSHING: Charles, Hugh 13-38; Ellis, Byron 4-7; Klatt, Joel 1-1; Vickers,Lawrence 1-minus 1. Texas-Young, Vince 10-58; Young, Selvin 19-43; Melton, Henry 8-15; Ogbonnaya, Chris 4-11; Hall, Ahmard 1-10; Charles, Jamaal 3-8; Taylor, Ramonce 1-4; TEAM 1-minus 4.

PASSING: Colorado-Klatt, Joel 19-39-1-189; Cox, James 2-5-0-3. Texas-Young, Vince 25-29-0-336; Nordgren, Matt 1-3-0-1.

RECEIVING: Colorado-Judge, Evan 6-37; Klopfenstein,Joe 5-60; Sprague, Dusty 3-39; Vickers,Lawrence 2-24; Williams,Patrick 2-17; Charles, Hugh 2-4; Sypniewski,Quinn 1-11. Texas-Sweed, Limas 7-88; Thomas, David 5-64; Taylor, Ramonce 5-14; Pittman, Billy 3-99; Carter, Brian 3-49; Young, Selvin 2-16; Jones, Nate 1-7.

INTERCEPTIONS: Colorado-None. Texas-Ross, Aaron 1-5.

FUMBLES: Colorado-Sprague, Dusty 1-0; Judge, Evan 1-1. Texas-Taylor, Ramonce 1-1; Ross, Aaron 1-0.

Stadium: Royal-Texas Memorial
Attendance: 83,474

A LESSON IN TEXAS FOOTBALL

Texas 52, Texas Tech 17 • Game 7, Oct. 22, 2005

AUSTIN, Texas — They came into the game undefeated, ranked in the top 10 in the country and featuring the nation's most explosive offense. But the Texas Tech Red Raiders were still no match for the Texas Longhorns.

The Longhorns put the brakes on Texas Tech's high-flying offense and sent the Red Raiders to their first loss of the season with a 52–17 beating before 83,919 fans at Royal-Memorial Stadium — the third-largest home crowd in Texas history.

"We basically just came out and tried to play Texas football," Texas wide receiver Ramonce Taylor said. "It felt great to put up 52 points against a team that has been putting up 70 and 80 points."

Texas quarterback Vince Young threw for two touchdowns and ran for another score as the Longhorns improved to 7–0 for the first time since 1983 with their 14th consecutive victory.

Longhorns coach Mack Brown, who the week prior had said he believed his team was among the best in the nation, was so impressed by Texas' performance that he took another step.

"Now I think this team definitely deserves to be No. 2 in the country," he said.

Texas Tech quarterback Cody Hodges, who threw for 643 yards against Kansas State the week before, went 42-for-64 for 369 yards, but the Red Raiders had trouble finding the end zone and stopping Texas' offense from doing so.

"This team continues to impress us as a staff,"

Brown said. "Our guys were excited about this game. But we are still a work in progress and we have the ability to play much better than we have yet. If you don't play your best game and you are still able to score 52 points, you know you have a special team out there. This is such a great win for the Longhorns."

Texas didn't allow Tech's high-powered offense to get off the ground, withstanding a flurry of short passes and taking advantage of a critical second-quarter stretch that turned a 10–10 tie into a 38–10 blowout. UT turned six consecutive possessions into touchdowns.

The Red Raiders, who were averaging a national-best 53.7 points and were second in total offense (572.8 yards per game), were uncharacteristically conservative at times and buckled under the Longhorns' pressure.

"Our offense scores 40 and 50 points a game," Texas safety Michael Huff said. "It's our job to go out there and get the ball back to our offense and let them do what they do."

Young, coming off perhaps the best game of his stellar career in the win over Colorado, tossed two early interceptions, but still threw for 239 yards on 12-of-22 passing. He also ran for 45 yards on seven carries, including a 10-yard touchdown run in the third quarter that made it 45–17.

"I was getting frustrated," Young said. "But I went off to the side. I put myself in a corner and just talked

Is that a Heisman pose? Young stated his case against the unbeaten Red Raiders.

to myself and tried to get ready for the next series."

Texas Tech led 7–3 – the Longhorns' first deficit since the second game of the season against Ohio State – and the game was tied 10–10 early in the second quarter. But Texas turned to a hurry-up, no-huddle offense, triggering 28 straight points that put the game away.

"Texas is the No. 2 team in the nation for a reason," Hodges said. "When you play against them you have to eliminate the margin for mental mistakes and turning over the ball. We shot ourselves in the foot early on offense and we were playing catch-up for the rest of the game."

Selvin Young rushed for a season-high 77 yards for the Longhorns and scored on touchdown runs of 10 and seven yards. Billy Pittman had three catches for 138 yards and two touchdowns, including a 75-yarder.

"Early in the first half, the safeties kept rolling down so I told Vince to give me a seam route and it was open," Pittman said.

The Horns capitalized on terrific special-teams play, getting a 38-yard punt return by Quan Cosby to Tech's eight to set up a one-yard touchdown run by Henry Melton. Tech trailed only 17–10 when Texas safety Michael Griffin blocked a punt, setting up Vince Young's 15-yard touchdown pass to Pittman.

After intercepting Hodges, Texas got a 48-yard pass from Young to Pittman and took a 31–10 half-time lead on Selvin Young's second touchdown run of the game, this one from seven yards out.

Tech QB Cody Hodges got his yards, but he paid a steep price.

"I would have to say that this is the best Texas team that I have been involved in playing against," Texas Tech coach Mike Leach said. "As the margin of error gets narrow, it becomes more and more important to do your job. A lot of the credit goes to Texas in the way they came out ready to play today.

"Texas is a great team. Most teams you average 15 plays per drive, where with Texas they will limit you to seven. You have to execute extra plays in order to be successful, and Texas made that hard for us today.

"When they got in those situations Texas rose up and did their job. They would find a way to make the big play or keep doing they things they were doing. I think they are very capable of winning a national championship." ■

Texas vs. Texas Tech

Score by Quarters	1	2	3	4	Score	
Texas Tech	7	3	7	0	17	Record: (6-1, 3-1)
Texas	10	21	14	7	52	Record: (7-0, 4-0)

Scoring Summary:

1st 10:40 UT Pino, David 40 yd field goal, 6-21 2:24, TT 0 - UT 3
    05:08 TT Henderson,T. 3 yd pass from Hodges, Cody (Trlica,Alex kick), 4-21 1:48, TT 7 - UT 3
    01:12 UT Melton, Henry 1 yd run (Pino, David kick), 3-8 1:23, TT 7 - UT 10

2nd 11:11 TT Trlica, Alex 32 yd field goal, 14-65 5:01, TT 10 - UT 10
    08:58 UT Young, Selvin 10 yd run (Pino, David kick), 7-80 2:13, TT 10 - UT 17
    06:41 UT Pittman, Billy 15 yd pass from Young, Vince (Pino, David kick), 2-23 0:11, TT 10 - UT 24
    01:57 UT Young, Selvin 7 yd run (Pino, David kick), 4-88 0:49, TT 10 - UT 31

3rd 13:42 UT Pittman, Billy 75 yd pass from Young, Vince (Pino, David kick), 3-80 1:18, TT 10 - UT 38
    08:39 TT Filani, Joel 6 yd pass from Hodges, Cody (Trlica,Alex kick), 15-80 5:03, TT 17 - UT 38
    04:15 UT Young, Vince 10 yd run (Pino, David kick), 11-65 4:24, TT 17 - UT 45

4th 06:30 UT Ogbonnaya, Chris 22 yd run (Pino, David kick), 2-26 0:51, TT 17 - UT 52

	TT	UT
FIRST DOWNS	29	21
RUSHES-YARDS (NET)	29-99	40-205
PASSING YDS (NET)	369	239
Passes Att-Comp-Int	64-42-1	22-12-2
TOTAL OFFENSE PLAYS-YARDS	93-468	62-444
Fumble Returns-Yards	0-0	0-0
Punt Returns-Yards	1-6	5-123
Kickoff Returns-Yards	5-88	2-67
Interception Returns-Yards	2-39	1-0
Punts (Number-Avg)	7-33.4	3-36.7
Fumbles-Lost	1-1	1-0
Penalties-Yards	10-78	3-35
Possession Time	36:01	23:59
Third-Down Conversions	5 of 16	5 of 10
Fourth-Down Conversions	2 of 3	0 of 1
Red-Zone Scores-Chances	3-4	5-6
Sacks By: Number-Yards	0-0	6-51

RUSHING: Texas Tech-Henderson, Taurean. 17-86; Hodges, Cody 12-13. Texas-Young, Selvin 16-77; Young, Vince 7-45; Charles, Jamaal 7-39; Ogbonnaya, Chris 3-26; Melton, Henry 6-12; Taylor, Ramonce 1-6.

PASSING: Texas Tech-Hodges, Cody 42-64-1-369. Texas-Young, Vince 12-22-2-239.

RECEIVING: Texas Tech-Filani, Joel 9-82; Johnson, Robert 9-76; Henderson,Taurean 8-59; Amendola, Danny 6-60; Hicks, Jarrett 5-63; Olomua, Bristol 3-28; Johnson, M. 1-2; Morris, Eric 1-minus 1. Texas-Taylor, Ramonce 5-66; Pittman, Billy 3-138; Carter, Brian 3-24; Cosby, Quan 1-11.

INTERCEPTIONS: Texas Tech-Naziruddin, K. 1-2; Parker, Chris 1-37. Texas-Crowder, Tim 1-0.

FUMBLES: Texas Tech-Henderson,Taurean 1-1. Texas-Melton, Henry 1-0.

Stadium: Royal-Texas Memorial
Attendance: 83,919

ESCAPE FROM STILLWATER

Texas 47, Oklahoma State 28 · Game 8, Oct. 29, 2005

STILLWATER, Okla. – Backed into a corner by Oklahoma State for the second year in a row, the Texas Longhorns – more specifically, quarterback Vince Young – came out swinging just in time to save the season.

Young broke free for an 80-yard touchdown run on the third play of the third quarter to spark to the Longhorns to 35 unanswered second-half points and a 47–28 win over the Cowboys at Boone Pickens Stadium.

"This was a wide-awakening for us," Texas free safety Michael Griffin said. "We came out with too much swagger."

Only a week after Missouri's Brad Smith became the first player in Division I-A history to have at least 230 yards rushing and passing in one game, Young matched the feat with a career-high 267 yards rushing and 239 passing.

"They did a lot of different things to us in the first half," said Young, whose previous career-high rushing total was 192 yards against Michigan in the Rose Bowl. "Our guys kept their poise. Nobody got rattled."

The Longhorns had just passed defending national champion USC earlier in the week for the top spot in the Bowl Championship Series, only to fall behind the Cowboys 28–9 midway through the second quarter.

Texas, which rallied from a 35–7 deficit last year to beat Oklahoma State 56–35 in Austin, scored touchdowns on five of its first seven possessions in the second half to rally for the improbable victory.

"We have been there before," Texas coach Mack Brown said. "I told the guys that we would probably fall behind, because Oklahoma State would play relaxed and they had nothing to lose.

"It was a trap game for us. I did not tell them that, but we have played three really emotional games in a row, and Oklahoma State had not played well and they read all week they had no chance."

Young had 133 yards rushing on 12 carries in the first half, but he committed two turnovers. Oklahoma State scored a pair of first-half touchdowns on passes from Al Pena to D'Juan Woods.

"They started off doing a lot of different things dropping guys and covering well," Young said. "I had to choose if I would throw it away or run with it. I would rather run with it than throw it away. Their game plan was to protect the pass and that gave me different areas to improve on. I took it upon myself and let my legs do a lot of the work."

The Cowboys caught the Longhorns off-guard on a fourth-and-one on their second possession when they broke the huddle quickly with three backs, snapped the ball immediately and Pena faked a handoff to Julius Crosslin up the middle before tossing a 49-yard touchdown pass to Woods, who was 15 yards beyond the nearest defender.

The Longhorns answered with a 20-yard touch-

David Thomas opened the scoring for Texas with a 20-yard TD catch.

down pass from Young to David Thomas, but had to settle for six points after the extra point was blocked. Crosslin's four-yard touchdown run with 2:50 left in the first quarter made it 14–6, and the Cowboys scored on the first play following an interception to take a 21–6 lead.

After a Young fumble late in the first half, Pena zipped a pass to Luke Frazier, but it was deflected into the air and Woods snagged it with his right hand and scooted into the end zone for a 30-yard score and a 28–9 Cowboys lead.

With Texas trailing 28–12, Brown told Young at the half that he had to take the game on his shoulders.

"That is his job and when he wants someone to step up, he will let you know," Young said. "He wanted more out of me, so I talked to my guys on the sideline to back me up and that is exactly what they did.

"He told me to go out there and make some plays and that everything would be all right, and that is exactly what we did. When the head coach trusts us like he does, that brings your confidence up, too."

Young got things going with an 80-yard touchdown run on the third play of the second half and added an eight-yard touchdown run late in the third quarter to bring the Longhorns within 28–26. He then found tight end Neale Tweedie open for his first career score on a 21-yard post pattern to give Texas a 34–28 lead.

With the UT backfield riddled with injuries and cramps – Jamaal Charles, Selvin Young and Chris Ogbonnaya limped off the field in the second half –

Ramonce Taylor took over the in fourth quarter when the Longhorns needed him most, scoring on runs of 57 and 12 yards.

Young took over to finish with a school-record 506 yards of total offense. UT had 606 yards overall.

"We just had to play our game," Young said. "We had two turnovers in the first half and a lot of opportunities that we just did not finish. We came out in the second half and played our game."

Ramonce Taylor scored on touchdown runs of 57 and 12 yards in the fourth quarter.

"We had a couple of running backs go down and coach told me to go in there," Taylor said. "I went in and tried to do the best I could and the outcome came out good. The offensive line blocked well for me. I read certain holes, cut back and took it up the field for the touchdown. Their cornerback is a fast guy, and I did not want to let him catch me, so I had to turn it on another notch."

As did the rest of the Longhorns during their escape from Stillwater. ■

Texas vs. Oklahoma State

Score by Quarters	1	2	3	4	Score	
Texas	9	3	22	13	47	Record: (8-0, 5-0)
Oklahoma State	21	7	0	0	28	Record: (3-5, 0-5)

Scoring Summary:

1st 09:45 OS   Woods, D'Juan 49 yd pass from Pena, Al (Redden, Bruce kick), 4-58 2:02, UT 0 - OS 7
    06:08 UT   Thomas, David 20 yd pass from Young, Vince (Pino, David kick blocked), 11-62 3:37, UT 6 - OS 7
    02:50 OS   Crosslin, Julius 4 yd run (Redden, Bruce kick), 9-76 3:18, UT 6 - OS 14
    02:27 OS   Pena, Al 17 yd run (Redden, Bruce kick), 1-17 0:05, UT 6 - OS 21
    01:21 UT   Pino, David 45 yd field goal, 6-52 1:06, UT 9 - OS 21

2nd 05:44 OS   Woods, D'Juan 29 yd pass from Pena, Al (Redden, Bruce kick), 2-29 0:09, UT 9 - OS 28
    00:00 UT   Pino, David 21 yd field goal, 14-35 5:44, UT 12 - OS 28

3rd 14:08 UT   Young, Vince 80 yd run (Pino, David kick), 3-80 0:52, UT 19 - OS 28
    02:23 UT   Young, Vince 8 yd run (Pino, David kick), 10-75 3:18, UT 26 - OS 28
    00:48 UT   Tweedie, Neale 21 yd pass from Young, Vince (Hall, Ahmard pass from Young, Vince), 4-59 0:25, UT 34 - OS 28

4th 09:26 UT   Taylor, Ramonce 57 yd run (Young, Vince pass failed), 2-63 0:50, UT 40 - OS 28
    03:39 UT   Taylor, Ramonce 12 yd run (Pino, David kick), 8-58 4:41, UT 47 - OS 28

	UT	OS
FIRST DOWNS	22	20
RUSHES-YARDS (NET)	49-367	46-250
PASSING YDS (NET)	239	152
Passes Att-Comp-Int	31-15-1	27-12-0
TOTAL OFFENSE PLAYS-YARDS	80-606	73-402
Fumble Returns-Yards	0-0	0-0
Punt Returns-Yards	2-23	1-32
Kickoff Returns-Yards	3-73	7-114
Interception Returns-Yards	0-0	1-21
Punts (Number-Avg)	2-38.0	7-33.4
Fumbles-Lost	1-1	1-1
Penalties-Yards	9-60	9-80
Possession Time	30:46	29:14
Third-Down Conversions	8 of 17	3 of 15
Fourth-Down Conversions	2 of 4	2 of 3
Red-Zone Scores-Chances	4-4	2-3
Sacks By: Number-Yards	1-15	2-9

RUSHING: Texas-Young, Vince 21-267; Taylor, Ramonce 5-71; Charles, Jamaal 7-20; Ogbonnaya, Chris 4-6; Melton, Henry 4-5; Young, Selvin 6-4; Nordgren, Matt 2-minus 6. Oklahoma State-Hamilton, Mike 31-194; Pena, Al 5-19; Gold, Greg 4-15; Devereaux, Tommy 2-8; Willis, Shawn 2-8; Crosslin, Julius 2-6.

PASSING: Texas-Young, Vince 15-30-1-239; Nordgren, Matt 0-1-0-0. Oklahoma State-Pena, Al 12-27-0-152.

RECEIVING: Texas-Thomas, David 6-104; Pittman, Billy 3-39; Tweedie, Neale 2-49; Charles, Jamaal 1-23; Taylor, Ramonce 1-13; Carter, Brian 1-7; Young, Selvin 1-4. Oklahoma State-Woods, D'Juan 4-90; Price, Ricky 2-22; Gold, Greg 2-7; Williams, Kenny 1-15; Pettigrew, Brandon 1-11; Devereaux, Tommy 1-7; Johnson, John 1-0.

INTERCEPTIONS: Texas-None. Oklahoma State-McLemore, Daniel 1-21.

FUMBLES: Texas-Young, Vince 1-1. Oklahoma State-Hamilton, Mike 1-1.

Stadium: Boone Pickens Stadium
Attendance: 48,035

ANOTHER STRATOSPHERE

Texas 62, Baylor 0 • Game 9, Nov. 5, 2005

WACO, Texas – In a season filled with impressive blowout victories and unforgettable individual performances, the Texas Longhorns somehow managed to kick their game into an even higher gear.

Receiver-turned-tailback Ramonce Taylor rushed for 102 yards and three touchdowns and hauled in a 42-yard touchdown pass from Vince Young as the Longhorns blasted Baylor 62–0 at Floyd Casey Stadium.

Taylor, a sophomore, became the third different starting tailback for Texas this season. A former high school running back, Taylor filled in for Selvin Young and Jamaal Charles, who were limited in practice with injuries.

"The best thing about today was that we played a more complete game," Texas coach Mack Brown said. "We've been playing halves or three quarters but today we came out and dominated for three quarters and then our other guys took over and we were still able to make plays."

Vince Young, who improved to 26–2 as a starter, had 351 total yards in just over three quarters on the field. He was 16-of-27 passing for 298 yards and two touchdowns and ran for 53 yards on eight carries.

"Perfect is hard to get but we did a great job today," Young said. "We came out to win the game and we expected to win. We had a great game today, the offense, defense and special teams all played great. We're going to keep playing hard. We

hope we made a statement to the bowl voters today."

Texas stretched its winning streak to 16 games, the second-longest in the nation behind No. 1 USC. The Longhorns have won eight in a row against Baylor, outscoring the Bears 203–14 the last four games, including three shutouts.

The Longhorns amassed 645 yards of total offense, the fifth-highest total in school history, while holding the Bears to just 201 yards.

"We came out and played our game," Young said. "We had a good week in practice and we came out and did our job. The offensive line did a great job opening up some holes. They do a great job of protecting me and opening up a lot of different receivers. We started off slow on offense but we pulled it together."

The Longhorns turned the ball over on downs on their first possession before turning a Baylor interception into a four-yard touchdown run by Charles. Texas settled for a 6–0 lead after David Pino missed the extra point.

Despite driving 44 yards in 11 plays, the Longhorns were forced to punt on their next possession, but it was only a matter of time before the Longhorns got rolling. Texas scored touchdowns on its last three drives of the first half to take a 27–0 halftime lead.

"Vince is as good as anyone in the country and he does it every week," Brown said. "I think his

Quan Cosby was one of many stars, scoring on a 55-yard hookup with Vince Young.

Baylor's only chance to score was snuffed with a blocked field goal by Robert Killebrew.

biggest disadvantage is he makes it look so easy. To have over 600 yards two weeks in a row is pretty special."

On Texas' first offensive snap after halftime, Young faked a handoff to Taylor and rolled to his right. Taylor raced downfield and caught a 42-yard pass, performing a dive into the end zone with no Baylor defender within 15 yards for a 34–0 Texas lead.

Brown gave Taylor a brief lecture on the sideline for his showboating.

"I told him I didn't appreciate it, and I didn't like it," Brown said. "I told him it's great to be back home, but that's not who we are, not how we act. He said, 'You're right.' That was the correct response."

Taylor also apologized to his teammates.

"I apologized to the team on the sideline because I was making it about me, and this is a team," he said.

The Longhorns scored on their first five possessions of the second half, including streak-of-lightning scoring drives of one, four and five plays.

"Baylor started well, but we started with a different attitude," Brown said. "Our fans are great here, and today was by far the best game we've had from our fans. It definitely makes a difference for our players and it has to be hard for the Baylor players. This was like a home game for us."

With the Longhorns up 55–0 having already amassed 546 of their 645 total yards, Young and Taylor were pulled. Seldom-used senior quarterback Matt Nordgren took over and scored the final touchdown on a 15-yard run in which he fumbled the ball and had it bounce back into his hands on

Another ruthlessly efficient day from Vince Young: 16-of-27, 298 yards, two TDs.

the way to the end zone.

Terrance Parks, who got his second career start at quarterback for Baylor in place of Shawn Bell, threw for only 89 yards and was intercepted twice.

"Texas is pretty good, there's no question about that," Baylor coach Guy Morriss said. "We lost our composure, but that's what good football teams do to you. We knew they were good, but I didn't think we would get dominated that bad on both sides of the ball."

Baylor's best scoring chance came in the third quarter, but Ryan Havens' 30-yard field-goal attempt was blocked by Robert Killebrew.

"We responded to a sub-par outing last week," Texas co-defensive coordinator Gene Chizik said. "We know we're good enough to get shutouts. We still think there is some room for improvement." ▪

Texas vs. Baylor

Score by Quarters	1	2	3	4	Score	
Texas	6	21	21	14	62	Record: (9-0, 6-0)
Baylor		0	0	0	0	Record: (4-5, 1-5)

Scoring Summary:

1st 09:17 UT   Charles, Jamaal 4 yd run (Pino, David kick failed), 5-68 1:34, UT 6 - BU 0

2nd 11:46 UT   Melton, Henry 1 yd run (Pino, David kick), 4-32 1:40, UT 13 - BU 0
02:58 UT   Charles, Jamaal 7 yd run (Pino, David kick), 14-80 5:48, UT 20 - BU 0
01:27 UT   Taylor, Ramonce 9 yd run (Pino, David kick), 2-38 0:31, UT 27 - BU 0

3rd 12:43 UT   Taylor, Ramonce 42 yd pass from Young, Vince (Pino, David kick), 1-42 0:09, UT 34 - BU 0
04:22 UT   Taylor, Ramonce 3 yd run (Pino, David kick), 13-80 5:22, UT 41 - BU 0
02:13 UT   Cosby, Quan 55 yd pass from Young, Vince (Pino, David kick), 4-71 1:31, UT 48 - BU 0

4th 13:45 UT   Taylor, Ramonce 11 yd run (Pino, David kick), 5-92 1:17, UT 55 - BU 0
05:18 UT   Nordgren, Matt 15 yd run (Pino, David kick), 11-67 6:28, UT 62 - BU 0

	UT	BU
FIRST DOWNS	35	13
RUSHES-YARDS (NET)	54-347	30-112
PASSING YDS (NET)	298	89
Passes Att-Comp-Int	27-16-0	23-10-2
TOTAL OFFENSE PLAYS-YARDS	81-645	53-201
Fumble Returns-Yards	0-0	0-0
Punt Returns-Yards	4-67	0-0
Kickoff Returns-Yards	0-0	6-140
Interception Returns-Yards	2-11	0-0
Punts (Number-Avg)	1-35.0	8-47.2
Fumbles-Lost	3-0	0-0
Penalties-Yards	8-93	10-77
Possession Time	35:27	24:33
Third-Down Conversions	10 of 14	2 of 13
Fourth-Down Conversions	2 of 3	0 of 0
Red-Zone Scores-Chances	6-6	0-1
Sacks By: Number-Yards	2-16	0-0

RUSHING: Texas-Taylor, Ramonce 15-102; Charles, Jamaal 13-72; Melton, Henry 13-62; Young, Vince 8-53; Nordgren, Matt 2-31; Houston, Michael 3-27. Baylor-Whitaker, Brand 8-49; Mosley, Paul 9-23; Price, Mario 1-17; Parks, Terrance 9-14; Jones, Jacoby 3-9.

PASSING: Texas-Young, Vince 16-27-0-298. Baylor-Parks, Terrance 10-23-2-89.

RECEIVING: Texas-Pittman, Billy 3-60; Taylor, Ramonce 3-43; Thomas, David 3-28; Cosby, Quan 2-79; Sweed, Limas 2-67; Jones, Nate 2-15; Charles, Jamaal 1-6. Baylor-Zeigler, Dominique 4-27; Shelton, Trent 2-11; Whitaker, Brandon 1-21; Rochon, Shaun 1-13; Sims, Carl 1-11; Baker, Mikail 1-6.

INTERCEPTIONS: Texas-Huff, Michael 1-11; Griffin, Michael 1-0. Baylor-None.

FUMBLES: Texas-Nordgren, Matt 1-0; Melton, Henry 1-0; Young, Vince 1-0. Baylor-None.

Stadium: Floyd Casey Stadium
Attendance: 44,783

THIS TIME, IT'S PERSONAL

Texas 66, Kansas 14 • Game 10, Nov. 12, 2005

AUSTIN, Texas – "Don't Mess with Texas."

Earlier in the week, quarterback Vince Young said he felt "disrespected" by Kansas coach Mark Mangino, who said the Jayhawks "outcoached and outplayed" Texas after the Longhorns' narrow 27–23 victory in 2004 in Lawrence, Kan.

"Kansas made me mad," Young said. "I'm really ticked off right now. That's just disrespectful. That's why I'm all riled up."

Word of advice: Don't make Young mad.

Young threw a career-high four touchdown passes as No. 2 Texas romped past Kansas 66–14 to clinch the Big 12 South Division title before a Senior Day sellout crowd of 83,696 at Royal-Texas Memorial Stadium.

"Talking about coaches and players ... we take that real personal," Young said. "That's like somebody talking about your mother."

Texas (10–0, 7–0 Big 12) ran its winning streak to 17 games and earned its first berth in the Big 12 championship game since 2001.

Kansas, which entered the game with the nation's No. 1-ranked run defense, was no match for the Longhorns. Texas held the Jayhawks to one first down in the first half, built a 52–0 halftime lead and rolled up 617 yards of total offense.

Texas scored at least 50 points for the sixth time this season and had outscored opponents 152–0 over eight quarters before Kansas scored on the first possession of the third quarter on Jon

Cornish's 59-yard run.

Young became Texas' career total offense leader with 8,269 yards, breaking the old mark of 8,059 set by Major Applewhite (1998-2001). Young passed for 264 yards and all four of his touchdowns in the first half, including long scoring strikes to Limas Sweed and Quan Cosby, before leaving with about five minutes left in the third quarter.

Ramonce Taylor had 96 rushing yards and scored on runs of 8 and 12 yards for the Longhorns.

"They disrespected us a little last year," Taylor said. "We took it to heart and came out and proved a point."

By halftime, UT led 52–0 and had clinched the South title with Texas Tech's 24–17 upset loss at Oklahoma State. The Horns finished with at least 600 yards of offense for the third consecutive week. UT had 336 of its 617 yards on the ground against the nation's stingiest run defense.

"When hitting on all cylinders, I think we're pretty good," Texas coach Mack Brown understated.

Brown said the Longhorns' performance had nothing to do with Mangino's comments after the 2004 matchup. Mangino was fined $5,000 for suggesting that the outcome of that game had been affected by the Bowl Championship Series. In particular, he implied that officials had made a pass interference call in Texas' favor with about two minutes remaining to help them win the game.

"We knew their whole focus was to stop the run,"

How do you like me now? Vince Young felt disrespected after Texas' win over Kansas in 2004. He took it out on the Jayhawks with four touchdown passes in 2005.

Brown said. "We thought we would throw the ball all over the place to show them that we were out there to win the game, not be stubborn. This was about us, not about them. It wasn't about comments made here or there, it was about winning the game."

Mangino offered his Heisman Trophy endorsement for Young after the game.

"I don't have a vote, but to me he looked like a Heisman Trophy guy," Mangino said.

Things began to unravel quickly for the Jayhawks. After punting on their first two possessions, the Longhorns scored a touchdown on seven of their next eight possessions. Texas scored 28 points in the first quarter, which included a 45-yard pass to Sweed and a 64-yard pass to Cosby, and added another 24 points in the second quarter punt.

UT caught a break when Kansas inside linebacker Kevin Kane was called for holding on Aaron Ross' second-quarter punt return to the Longhorns' 31-yard line. The Jayhawks were forced to punt again, and this time Ross took the ball up the middle and dodged two tacklers for a 71-yard touchdown return, his second of the season. The 52 first-half points tied the school record.

In one of their most dominating performances of the season, the Longhorns' defense forced Kansas to punt 11 times.

"We always feel like we have the best defense on the field," UT safety Michael Huff said.

The members of one of the most successful sen-

Young went deep with TD strikes of 45, 64 and 29 yards.

ior classes in school history were also able to go out as winners in their final appearance in Austin. After the game, several players ran around the field as fans waved red roses amid chants of "Rose Bowl."

Texas needs a win over Texas A&M on Nov. 25 to complete the school's first unbeaten regular season since 1983.

"We're just taking care of business," Young said. Not to mention getting some respect. ■

Texas vs. Kansas

Score by Quarters	1	2	3	4	Score	
Kansas	0	0	14	0	14	Record: (5-5, 2-5)
Texas	28	24	7	7	66	Record: (10-0, 7-0)

Scoring Summary:

1st 07:53 UT Sweed, Limas 45 yd pass from Young, Vince (Pino, David kick), 3-65 0:42, KU 0 - UT 7
    07:40 UT Charles, Jamaal 10 yd run (Pino, David kick), 1-10 0:13, KU 0 - UT 14
    04:38 UT Cosby, Quan 64 yd pass from Young, Vince (Pino, David kick), 3-81 1:06, KU 0 - UT 21
    02:29 UT Ross, Aaron 71 yd punt return (Pino, David kick), , KU 0 - UT 28

2nd 12:13 UT Taylor, Ramonce 8 yd run (Pino, David kick), 9-87 3:29, KU 0 - UT 35
    10:19 UT Thomas, David 29 yd pass from Young, Vince (Pino, David kick), 3-47 0:45, KU 0 - UT 42
    04:13 UT Ullman, Peter 3 yd pass from Young, Vince (Pino, David kick), 1-3 0:06, KU 0 - UT 49
    00:55 UT Pino, David 35 yd field goal, 9-54 1:44, KU 0 - UT 52

3rd 14:14 KU Cornish, Jon 59 yd run (Webb, Scott kick), 2-65 0:46, KU 7 - UT 52
    06:41 UT Taylor, Ramonce 12 yd run (Pino, David kick), 15-80 7:33, KU 7 - UT 59
    03:34 KU McAnderson, Brandon 15 yd run (Webb, Scott kick), 2-28 0:14, KU 14 - UT 59

4th 14:53 UT Young, Selvin 21 yd run (Phillips, Kyle kick), 8-78 3:41, KU 14 - UT 66

	KU	UT
FIRST DOWNS	9	29
RUSHES-YARDS (NET)	22-119	53-336
PASSING YDS (NET)	148	281
Passes Att-Comp-Int	35-17-1	28-19-1
TOTAL OFFENSE PLAYS-YARDS	57-267	81-617
Fumble Returns-Yards	0-0	0-0
Punt Returns-Yards	2-10	4-91
Kickoff Returns-Yards	7-116	1-21
Interception Returns-Yards	1-18	1-31
Punts (Number-Avg)	11-42.6	5-35.4
Fumbles-Lost	1-1	3-0
Penalties-Yards	8-55	6-35
Possession Time	25:34	34:26
Third-Down Conversions	2 of 15	7 of 14
Fourth-Down Conversions	0 of 1	0 of 0
Red-Zone Scores-Chances	1-2	5-5
Sacks By: Number-Yards	1-12	2-17

RUSHING: Kansas-Green, Clark 11-69; Cornish, Jon 6-57; McAnderson, Brandon 1-15; Gordon, Charles 1-1; Swanson, Jason 3-minus 23. Texas-Taylor, Ramonce 14-96; Melton, Henry 7-73; Charles, Jamaal 8-70; Young, Selvin 7-57; McCoy, Matt 1-25; Hobbs, Antwaun 7-17; Nordgren, Matt 1-2; Myers, Marcus 1-1; TEAM 1-minus 1; Young, Vince 6-minus 4.

PASSING: Kansas-Swanson, Jason 17-35-1-148. Texas-Young, Vince 19-27-0-281; Nordgren, Matt 0-1-1-0.

RECEIVING: Kansas-Gordon, Charles 6-47; Herford, Marcus 4-30; Foster, Jeff 2-45; Henry, Marcus 1-18; Fine, Derek 1-7; Roux, Dominic 1-6; Green, Clark 1-0; Cornish, Jon 1-minus 5. Texas-Thomas, David 4-76; Pittman, Billy 4-39; Sweed, Limas 3-69; Jones, Nate 2-12; Cosby, Quan 1-64; Gatewood, Tyrell 1-9; Taylor, Ramonce 1-5; Ullman, Peter 1-3; Hall, Ahmard 1-3; Charles, Jamaal 1-1.

INTERCEPTIONS: Kansas-Kane, Kevin 1-18. Texas-Ross, Aaron 1-31.

FUMBLES: Kansas-Heaggans, Greg 1-1. Texas-Young, Vince 1-0; Sweed, Limas 1-0; Taylor, Ramonce 1-0.

Stadium: Royal-Texas Memorial
Attendance: 83,696

SIGH OF RELIEF

Texas 40, Texas A&M 29 • Game 11, Nov. 25, 2005

COLLEGE STATION, Texas — Just two wins shy of playing for their first national championship since 1969, the Texas Longhorns had the unusual task of waiting until the fourth quarter before breathing a sigh of relief.

Having blown out all but two of their first 10 opponents, the Longhorns kept their perfect season alive with a hard-fought 40–29 victory over rival Texas A&M before 86,617 fans at Kyle Field.

"It was a great eye-opener," Texas co-defensive coordinator Gene Chizik said. "Today became a day of scrambling and adjusting. The bottom line is we're 11–0."

Texas quarterback Vince Young saw his Heisman Trophy hopes take a significant blow with his shakiest game of the season, but he still made enough plays to give the Longhorns their 18th consecutive victory.

"I think I was the only one in the country who anticipated this," Texas coach Mack Brown said. "I told the guys, they're going to pull it all out because they've got nothing to lose. I was really, really not proud of myself that I was right."

With the Longhorns leading by only eight points in the fourth quarter, Texas defensive tackle Rod Wright stripped the ball from Texas A&M backup quarterback Stephen McGee at the Longhorns' 10-yard line with 5:13 left in the game.

The Longhorns put the game away with 2:22 remaining when David Pino, who missed wide right on a 33-yard attempt earlier in the quarter, booted a 29-yard field goal that put Texas ahead 40–29.

"They played their hearts out," Wright said of the Aggies. "They ran a whole lot of options and the quarterback was able to scramble. He's a fast guy and we weren't tackling well. Basically, they just put a lot of pressure on us. And we didn't answer for a while."

The victory gave the Longhorns their first 11–0 regular season since 1983, as Texas finished the regular season undefeated for the 13th time in school history.

"This is one of the toughest places to play in the country," Brown said. "We didn't play very well in the first half. Credit Texas A&M for playing so hard. They had a good plan. I thought their fans were great, just like they always are. Give our football team credit for not panicking with all that's on the line. We did the things we needed to do to win. It's so hard to go 11–0 anymore."

Going against the 109th-ranked defense in the country, Young passed for just 162 yards, rushed for 19 yards and committed two turnovers that led directly to Aggie touchdowns.

"They gave us all they had," Young said. "Our defense came up with big turnovers. All that matters to me is that we won. I think I did a good job of managing the game. We got a 'W.' We spread the ball around pretty good and got the ball in different people's hands. We didn't play as good as we've been playing."

Young proved himself as an escape artist with Texas' come-from-behind win over an inspired group of Aggies.

McGee, a freshman, got the start in place of the injured senior Reggie McNeal and kept the Aggies in the game by rushing for 108 yards and two touchdowns. Freshman running back Jorvorskie Lane, a load at 265 pounds, added 104 bruising yards on 17 carries.

"It leaves a bad taste in your mouth," Wright said. "When you give up over 200 yards rushing, you don't want to think about it. You just want to take it and throw it out."

The Longhorns, who were outgained 395–336, took advantage of an interception and short punt to take a 14–0 lead. The Aggies cut the lead to 14–9 when Lane threw a halfback touchdown pass to Jason Carter to end the first quarter.

"We didn't always execute perfectly but you know as a team we hung in there and fought and we had a lot of people's help," McGee said.

The teams swapped scores and lead changes three times before the Longhorns took the lead for good on Ramonce Taylor's eight-yard run with 8:15 to play in the third quarter that put Texas ahead 28–22.

Cedric Griffin's 11-yard touchdown on a blocked punt return seemed to put the Longhorns in control with a 34–22 lead late in the third quarter, but McGee answered with a one-yard touchdown run to get the Aggies within 34–29.

"You're playing against a national championship-like effort every weekend because the other team

Rod Wright sealed the closer-than-expected win with a key strip.

wants to beat you so bad," Brown said. "I think this is the best possible thing that could have happened to us today because it got our guys' attention and it got our coaches' attention. Stephen did a great job. Give Texas A&M credit. This is a 112-year-old rivalry that means a whole lot to all these guys."

Texas took a 73–34–5 lead in the series, including 23–21–2 at Kyle Field. The Longhorns have won 14 consecutive Big 12 games and 21 of their previous 22 conference games. ■

Texas vs. Texas A&M

Score by Quarters	1	2	3	4	Score	
Texas	14	7	13	6	40	Record: (11-0, 8-0)
Texas A&M	9	6	14	0	29	Record: (5-6, 3-5)

Scoring Summary:

1st 07:40 UT Melton, Henry 8 yd run (Pino, David kick), 3-17 0:19, UT 7 - TA 0
    04:19 UT Taylor, Ramonce 5 yd run (Pino, David kick), 7-48 1:56, UT 14 - TA 0
    00:22 TA Pegram, Todd 31 yd field goal, 12-67 3:57, UT 14 - TA 3
    00:04 TA Carter, Jason 35 yd pass from Lane, Jorvorskie (Pegram, Todd pass intcpt), 1-35 0:07, UT 14 - TA 9

2nd 09:26 TA Leone, Brandon 16 yd run (Lane, Jorvorskie rush fumbled), 7-85 3:51, UT 14 - TA 15
    03:55 UT Hall, Ahmard 14 yd pass from Young, Vince (Pino, David kick), 7-77 2:44, UT 21 - TA 15

3rd 12:36 TA McGee, Stephen 11 yd run (Pegram, Todd kick), 2-15 0:53, UT 21 - TA 22
    08:15 UT Taylor, Ramonce 8 yd run (Pino, David kick), 10-80 4:21, UT 28 - TA 22
    05:45 UT Griffin, Cedric 11 yd blocked punt return (Pino, David kick failed), , UT 34 - TA 22
    02:09 TA McGee, Stephen 1 yd run (Pegram, Todd kick), 8-65 3:36, UT 34 - TA 29

4th 14:55 UT Pino, David 41 yd field goal, 6-56 2:14, UT 37 - TA 29
    02:22 UT Pino, David 29 yd field goal, 6-20 3:19, UT 40 - TA 29

	UT	TA
FIRST DOWNS	18	22
RUSHES-YARDS (NET)	42-174	52-277
PASSING YDS (NET)	162	118
Passes Att-Comp-Int	24-13-1	24-10-1
TOTAL OFFENSE PLAYS-YARDS	66-336	76-395
Fumble Returns-Yards	0-0	0-0
Punt Returns-Yards	2-25	1-0
Kickoff Returns-Yards	1-21	6-117
Interception Returns-Yards	1--2	1-17
Punts (Number-Avg)	3-33.7	5-27.2
Fumbles-Lost	4-2	4-2
Penalties-Yards	3-15	9-77
Possession Time	24:43	35:17
Third-Down Conversions	6 of 15	4 of 14
Fourth-Down Conversions	1 of 1	0 of 1
Red-Zone Scores-Chances	5-6	4-5
Sacks By: Number-Yards	4-45	3-32

RUSHING: Texas-Taylor, Ramonce 15-102; Melton, Henry 3-32; Young, Vince 11-19; Charles, Jamaal 5-10; Pittman, Billy 1-9; Bobino, Rashad 1-6; Young, Selvin 3-5; TEAM 3-minus 9. Texas A&M-McGee, Stephen 24-108; Lane, Jorvorskie 17-104; Lewis, Courtney 4-36; Leone, Brandon 6-31; Carter, Jason 1-1; Stutz, Boone 0-minus 3.

PASSING: Texas-Young, Vince 13-24-1-162. Texas A&M-McGee, Stephen 9-23-1-83; Lane, Jorvorskie 1-1-0-35.

RECEIVING: Texas-Thomas, David 3-37; Cosby, Quan 3-34; Sweed, Limas 3-32; Hall, Ahmard 2-39; Pittman, Billy 1-11; Taylor, Ramonce 1-9. Texas A&M-Mobley, DeQawn 3-30; Bennett, Martel 3-17; Carter, Jason 2-60; Leone, Brandon 1-6; Brown, Pierre 1-5.

INTERCEPTIONS: Texas-Kelson, Drew 1-minus 2. Texas A&M-Bullitt, Melvin 1-17.

FUMBLES: Texas-Young, Vince 2-1; Charles, Jamaal 1-1; Cosby, Quan 1-0. Texas A&M-McGee, Stephen 3-1; Carpenter, Marquis 1-1.

Stadium: Kyle Field
Attendance: 86,617

SENDING A MESSAGE

Texas 70, Colorado 3 • Game 12, Dec. 3, 2005

HOUSTON, Texas – Texas quarterback Vince Young refined his talents just a fly route away from Reliant Stadium at perennial Houston high school football power Madison.

Although he was highly recruited and posted gaudy prep numbers, Young was never able to play for a championship – something Young and the Longhorns earned the right to do by bashing Colorado in the Big 12 championship game.

Young's homecoming couldn't have gone any better as he accounted for four touchdowns to lead Texas to a 70–3 wipeout of the Buffaloes – the eighth-largest margin of victory in school history – for the Big 12 title.

"The whole week of practice, I was excited and pumped up," said Young, who had many family members in the stands. "It was pretty emotional. I was looking forward to coming home to family and friends and everybody."

When the final gun sounded, the Longhorns' players took the field with roses in hand and donned championship T-shirts.

Texas (12–0) will now turn its attention to the Rose Bowl, where it will face No. 1 USC on Jan. 4 for the national championship.

"We didn't play as well as we needed to or wanted to last Friday (at Texas A&M, a 40–29 win), and we didn't played as passionate as we'd like to, but the guys came out and were hitting on all cylinders today," Texas coach Mack Brown said. "We played a great football game and we're excited about going to Pasadena."

Young, coming off a sub-par performance against Texas A&M, helped his Heisman Trophy campaign by throwing for 193 yards on 14-of-17 passing with three touchdowns. He was pulled early in the third quarter with the game firmly in hand.

Young will now return to the site where he enjoyed his coming-out party in last year's scintillating victory over Michigan in the Rose Bowl.

"Going back there, and having fun like we did, I'm not going to do anything different," Young said. "Whatever got us to 12-0 right now, we want to keep it like that. We don't want to change nothing. Pretty much we want to go out there and have fun and take care of business."

Texas was never threatened in this game, taking a 14–0 lead in the first quarter and a 35–3 lead midway through the second quarter against a team they had already beaten 42–17 during the regular season.

"As a defense, before the game we talked about getting turnovers, and I think we got four or five, so that's great," said Texas defensive lineman Rodrique Wright, who also is from Houston. "Whenever we do that, our offense is going to put up a lot of points when we give them the ball, so that was our goal."

A week after struggling past Texas A&M, the Longhorns played virtually mistake-free football.

No doubt about it: The 2005 Longhorns were the class of the Big 12.

They rushed for 268 yards against the nation's No. 2 run defense, blocked a field-goal attempt, scored a touchdown off a blocked punt and held the Buffaloes to 191 yards of offense.

"We were upset about the rushing defense," Wright said of Texas' defensive performance against Texas A&M. "We took it upon ourselves, and the coaches pushed us a lot during scout periods to focus on stopping the run."

The Longhorns scored on 10 of their first 11 possessions, with no drive lasting more than nine plays. Texas rolled up 486 yards and got touchdowns from Henry Milton, Jamaal Charles, Vince Young, Limas Sweed, David Thomas, Selvin Young and Brandon Foster.

Colorado coach Gary Barnett, whose team lost its third game in a row, called the game "numbing."

"We knew Texas was going to beat us probably, but we were going to be able to get some points on the board," Barnett said. "Turnovers and penalties killed us. We continued to do that today. It certainly hurt our chances in this game."

The first few minutes did not hint at what was to come after Colorado easily moved the ball into Texas territory on its opening drive. But Longhorn safety Michael Huff knocked the ball loose from Hugh Charles on a pass completion and defensive end Brian Robison recovered the loose ball at the Texas 35. Robison also blocked a 31-yard field-goal attempt.

The Longhorns took control from there, using a no-huddle offense to wear down the Buffaloes. Texas scored four touchdowns in the final 12 minutes of the second quarter, including a two-yard run by Vince Young and a 31-yard catch by Sweed during a 23-second stretch.

Colorado scored its only points on a 25-yard field goal by Mason Crosby with 14:48 remaining in the second quarter.

Texas added four touchdowns during the first 7:24 of the second half. Selvin Young scored on a four-yard run, Michael Griffin blocked a punt that was recovered by Foster in the end zone, Jamaal Charles added a 26-yard touchdown run and Melton bulled in from a yard out.

"I thought not only the keys plays by the defense, but Vince throwing the ball deep today was a big difference in the game as well," Brown said. "He threw a couple of times over their heads and they made some huge plays.

"You never know what happens in the game like this when you've got the crowd and things aren't going well."

Texas won its 12 games by an average of 50.9–14.5. They scored at least 40 points in a game 11 times, reached 50 seven times, 60 four times and hit 70 in a game for the first time in a game since 1996.

"When I came to Texas, everybody said all we would like you to do is get us back in the top 10 where we're recognized as a great program again," Brown said. "We have been doing that the last four or five years.

"Texas is a factor. When you get to the end and don't finish it like you want to, it's really disappointing. But you can feel as a coach how close you are, and last year we took a big jump." ▪

Big 12 Championship

Score by Quarters	1	2	3	4	Score	
Texas	14	28	28	0	70	Record: (12-0, 8-0)
Colorado	0	3	0	0	3	Record: (7-5, 5-3)

Scoring Summary:

1st 09:44 UT   Melton, Henry 1 yd run (Pino, David kick), 7-65 1:56, UT 7 - CU 0
   05:59 UT   Charles, Jamaal 3 yd pass from Young, Vince (Pino, David kick), 8-52 3:19, UT 14 - CU 0

2nd 14:48 CU   Crosby, Mason 25 yd field goal, 4--3 0:19, UT 14 - CU 3
   12:00 UT   Young, Vince 2 yd run (Pino, David kick), 7-46 2:48, UT 21 - CU 3
   11:37 UT   Sweed, Limas 31 yd pass from Young, Vince (Pino, David kick), 1-31 0:07, UT 28 - CU 3
   07:20 UT   Thomas, David 8 yd pass from Young, Vince (Pino, David kick), 4-44 1:44, UT 35 - CU 3
   00:25 UT   Charles, Jamaal 2 yd run (Pino, David kick), 9-71 2:44, UT 42 - CU 3

3rd 11:26 UT   Young, Selvin 4 yd run (Pino, David kick), 8-68 3:34, UT 49 - CU 3
   10:21 UT   Foster, Brandon 0 yd blocked punt return (Pino, David kick), UT 56 - CU 3
   09:59 UT   Charles, Jamaal 26 yd run (Pino, David kick), 1-26 0:08, UT 63 - CU 3
   07:36 UT   Melton, Henry 1 yd run (Pino, David kick), 6-16 2:18, UT 70 - CU 3

	UT	CU
FIRST DOWNS	26	12
RUSHES-YARDS (NET)	57-268	26-82
PASSING YDS (NET)	218	109
Passes Att-Comp-Int	19-16-1	32-15-1
TOTAL OFFENSE PLAYS-YARDS	76-486	58-191
Fumble Returns-Yards	0-0	0-0
Punt Returns-Yards	4-42	1-3
Kickoff Returns-Yards	2-83	5-96
Interception Returns-Yards	1-11	1-21
Punts (Number-Avg)	2-34.0	7-32.6
Fumbles-Lost	0-0	4-3
Penalties-Yards	11-93	8-74
Possession Time	36:06	23:54
Third-Down Conversions	11 of 16	3 of 14
Fourth-Down Conversions	0 of 1	1 of 2
Red-Zone Scores-Chances	7-8	1-2
Sacks By: Number-Yards	0-0	0-0

RUSHING: Texas-Charles, Jamaal 7-62; Young, Vince 8-57; Young, Selvin 3-42; Taylor, Ramonce 14-41; Melton, Henry 13-34; McCoy, Matt 3-11; Ogbonnaya, Chris 5-11; Nordgren, Matt 2-9; Myers, Marcus 2-1. Colorado-Charles, Hugh 12-36; Klatt, Joel 4-26; Robinson,Stephone 1-9; Cox, James 2-6; Ellis, Byron 5-3; Vickers,Lawrence 2-2.

PASSING: Texas-Young, Vince 14-17-1-193; Nordgren, Matt 2-2-0-25. Colorado-Klatt, Joel 14-24-1-100; Cox, James 1-8-0-9.

RECEIVING: Texas-Sweed, Limas 5-102; Cosby, Quan 4-52; Thomas, David 3-31; Walker, George 1-22; Young, Selvin 1-5; Ogbonnaya, Chris 1-3; Charles, Jamaal 1-3. Colorado-Klopfenstein,Joe 4-23; Sypniewski, Quinn 2-15; Barnett, Alvin 2-14; Charles, Hugh 2-5; Judge, Evan 1-24; Sprague, Dusty 1-22; Williams, Patrick 1-5; Vickers, Lawrence 1-2; Ellis, Byron 1-minus 1.

INTERCEPTIONS: Texas-Brown, Tarell 1-11. Colorado-Hubbard, Tom 1-21.

FUMBLES: Texas-None. Colorado-Charles, Hugh 2-2; Klopfenstein,Joe 1-0; Klatt, Joel 1-1.

Stadium: Reliant
Attendance: 71,107

VINCE YOUNG • Quarterback

Though Reggie Bush fans may argue otherwise, Young may have been the most scintillating performer in college football this season. The Heisman runner-up led the nation's highest-scoring offense (50.9 ppg) with one jaw-dropping outing after another. In particular, his play in comeback wins over Ohio State and Oklahoma State showed the nation a toughness and resiliency that set him apart from every other quarterback in college football.

- Young led the nation in passing efficiency rating (168.8)

- Threw for 2,769 yards, with 26 touchdown passes

- Completed 63.9 percent of his passes

- Led the Longhorns in rushing with 850 yards

AP Wide World

QUARTERBACK FOR LIFE

Vince Young Silences His Critics Once and For All

Before the Texas Longhorns took off on one of the most memorable seasons in school history, Vince Young wanted to make one thing clear.

"I'm a quarterback for life," Young said.

The statement was in response to criticism that Young's future in the NFL would be as a wide receiver. Young shook his head in almost defiant disagreement when reminded about the talk that his throwing mechanics need work, his passes aren't crisp and his decision-making is sketchy.

That was in July.

By December, Young had made his case as one of the nation's top dual-threat quarterbacks in the country. He led the second-ranked Longhorns to an unbeaten regular season for the first time since 1983 and a spot in the Rose Bowl to play top-ranked USC for the national title.

He finished runner-up to USC tailback Reggie Bush for the Heisman Trophy. He won the Maxwell Award as the nation's top college football player.

The most satisfying piece of hardware he picked up on the awards banquet, however, might have been the Davey O'Brien National Quarterback Award.

"A lot of people doubted me about being a quarterback and that I should play another position," Young said. "I wanted to show the world I could be a good quarterback."

Young became the first UT quarterback to lead the nation in passing efficiency and set career highs in passing yards (2,769) and touchdowns

(26). He set a UT single-season record with 3,619 yards of total offense.

His 29–2 record as a starter – a .935 winning percentage in three seasons – is sixth-best all-time in NCAA history for a quarterback with a minimum of 25 career starts.

A year earlier, Young was an athletic 6-foot-5 player admittedly still learning the position. He threw nearly as many interceptions (11) as touchdown passes (12) and ranked 51st in the nation in passing efficiency.

"The only stat he's interested in is winning," UT coach Mack Brown said. "He sincerely believes that."

After a 12–0 loss to Oklahoma in 2004 – the Longhorns' fifth straight in the Red River Rivalry – Young heard whispers that he shouldn't even be a quarterback. He didn't listen, leading the Longhorns to improbable comebacks against Oklahoma State and Kansas before his national coming-out party against Michigan in the Rose Bowl. Against the Wolverines, Young rushed for four TDs and threw another in a 38–37 win.

This year the Longhorns went from no points against OU to 45, the most they've ever scored in 100 meetings against the Sooners.

"He'll be one of the great quarterbacks to ever play college football before he leaves Texas," Brown said. "I think he'll be in the (college) Hall of Fame and a pro quarterback if he keeps doing what he's doing."

Young embraces his role as the unquestioned leader of the Longhorns. He wears a while wristband on his left arm with the word "heart."

"I'm the guy and I'm going to be the leader," Young said. "That's my role."

Young spent the offseason attending 6 a.m. film sessions. He wrote on a grease board in the UT locker room: "Whoever wants to beat Ohio State meet me on the practice field at 7 p.m." for an informal workout. Nearly the entire team showed up. He is a leader in every sense of the word, keeping a loose atmosphere on the practice field and offering soothing words in the huddle even in the most desperate moments.

Just as much as he's improved reading defenses and making pre-snap decisions, Young said he is more relaxed at quarterback.

"Just to show the world, with all the negative things that have been said, that I can answer with my arm, I kind of got more respect," Young said. "Now people say I'm a quarterback and shouldn't be a receiver."

Who's going to argue? Not only is Young being mentioned as one of the greatest quarterbacks in UT history, but he added to his legacy by leading the Longhorns to one of the greatest seasons in school history.

When he took a blow to the head against Ohio State with the Longhorns trailing 22–16 late in the fourth quarter, Young bounced up and patted the Buckeye defender on the backside. A few plays later, Young connected on a 24-yard pass to Limas Sweed for the game-winner.

His signature moment also happened to save the Longhorns' season. With Texas trailing by as many as 19 points in the first half against Oklahoma State, Young went into what he calls "Jordan Mode." On the third play of the second half, Young pump-faked an Oklahoma State defender on the way to an 80-yard touchdown run. He finished the game with 506 total yards − 267 on the ground, 239 through the air − in a 47–28 win.

Young has accounted for 78 touchdowns in his career, breaking the school record of 76 set by Ricky Williams, the 1998 Heisman winner. His 8,705 yards of total offense is also a school record.

"I don't care what it takes to win. I'll run or pass," said Young, who also led the Longhorns in rushing with 850 yards this season.

Young is known for his loose attitude, leading the team in "flow sessions" before practice. His personality has even rubbed off on Brown and offensive coordinator Greg Davis.

Before a practice early in the season, Brown showed up with his sweatpants baggy and his cap turned sideways. "That's the way I get down," Brown said.

"He's really a big kid," Texas tackle Justin Blalock said of Young. "He likes to have fun, and he wants everyone else to have fun. If you don't know Vince, you won't understand him going around the locker room getting everyone pumped up."

Young is without doubt the most important player Brown has ever recruited at Texas and a player who has almost single-handedly changed the program forever.

"It's like we're best friends," Young said. "I thought our relationship would be good, but not as good as it is. He has let me grow into a man."

After a successful high school career that turned him into a Houston legend, Young's path now leads to the NFL. He put the rumors to rest in early October when he said he would return to Texas for his senior season in 2006.

Even after all the strides he made in 2005, all the critics he silenced and leading the Longhorns to the national title game couldn't hide Young's disappointment on Dec. 10 when he finished second to USC tailback Reggie Bush in the Heisman ceremony at Times Square.

"I'm just disappointed for my fans, especially my teammates and everyone back at home for not representing them the right way," Young said.

When he rejoined his teammates in Austin a few days later, Young was greeted by a standing ovation in the locker room.

"I wouldn't trade him for any other quarterback," receiver Billy Pittman said.

Emphasis on quarterback. ∎

JONATHAN SCOTT • Offensive Tackle

Scott is a four-year star at offensive tackle, a road-grader who has anchored an offensive line that paved the way for the nation's third-ranked rushing attack. At 6'7", 315 pounds, Scott has the size, the wingspan and the surprising quickness to provide the perfect bodyguard for Vince Young and the Longhorns' other offensive weapons.

Jonathan Scott paved the way for Cedric Benson last year and has been both an irresistible force as a run blocker and immovable object as a pass blocker for Vince Young and company this year.

RODRIQUE WRIGHT • Defensive Tackle

An indelible memory of the 2005 season: Wright, picking up a fumble and lumbering for a 67-yard touchdown against Oklahoma. On that one play, Texas exorcised its OU demons, and Wright established himself as one of the nation's great defensive playmakers. Of his 46 total tackles, 14 came behind the line of scrimmage, and he applied 15 quarterback pressures.

Rodrique Wright menaced opposing quarterbacks all season.

AP Wide World

MICHAEL HUFF • Safety

Huff has started 49 of his 50 games as a Longhorn, and in most of those 49 games, he has supplied at least one game-changing play. After he returned four interceptions for touchdowns in his first two seasons, teams learned not to throw in his direction. But he still supplied the Horns with this amazing statline in 2005: 97 tackles, two sacks, nine tackles for a loss, 13 passes broken up, four forced fumbles and an interception.

Michael Huff poses with the Jim Thorpe Award during the Home Depot 2005 College Football Awards at Walt Disney World. Huff won the Thorpe Award as the best defensive back in the country, becoming the first Longhorn player to do so.

RUNNING BACK BY COMMITTEE WORKS JUST FINE FOR TEXAS

AUSTIN, Texas – Entering the season, the Texas Longhorns had big shoes to fill.

Cedric Benson, the sixth all-time leading rusher in NCAA history with 5,540 yards, was earning a multi-million-dollar paycheck with the Chicago Bears in the NFL.

For the first time in a decade, there wasn't a dominant presence in the Texas backfield, unheard-of at a school that has produced Earl Campbell, Ricky Williams, Chris Gilbert, Roosevelt Leaks and Benson.

Instead, the Longhorns replaced Benson with a multi-dimensional sophomore, an injury-prone junior and a pair of true freshmen. Known as more of a pounding rushing team with Williams and Benson, the Longhorns suddenly became a team that could beat you inside and out.

During a record-setting offensive season that produced an average 50.9 points and 508.4 yards per game during a 12–0 regular season, the Longhorns did not skip a beat with their four-headed monster in the backfield. Texas averaged 273.8 yards on the ground, third-best in the nation and only 25 yards fewer per game than the previous season. They had six games with at least 300 yards on the ground.

Yet the Longhorns reached the national championship without producing a 1,000-yard rusher for the first time since 1994.

"It shows the strength and depth of this team," Texas coach Mack Brown said. "We don't have just one guy to carry the load."

Each member of the quartet brings something a little different to the offensive mix. But it is that multi-dimensional sophomore who has been mentioned in the loftiest company.

Ramonce Taylor is the kind of multi-dimensional threat the Longhorns have been looking for, and has drawn comparisons to Heisman Trophy winner Reggie Bush for his ability to line up in the backfield, receiver and on kickoffs. Taylor led the Longhorns with 1,181 all-purpose yards during the regular season – 501 rushing, 268 receiving and 412 on kickoff returns – and 14 touchdowns.

"Just to know he can break it any time, you've got to get that guy the ball," Texas quarterback Vince Young said.

During the offseason, Brown called Norm Chow, the former offensive coordinator at USC, to ask how he used Bush the last two years. The idea was to use Taylor at tailback in a split role with junior Selvin Young to begin the season. The emergence of true freshman Jamaal Charles, who had 350 yards in his first three collegiate games, gave Texas the flexibility of using Taylor more at receiver.

"When we saw how good Jamaal Charles was, that allowed us to see where we would move Ramonce, where would we put him," Brown said.

Charles rushed for 350 yards in the season's first three games, including 135 yards in the opener against Louisiana-Lafayette to set the school's

Ramonce Taylor

losing streak to the Sooners.

But injuries to Charles and Selvin Young throughout the season forced the Longhorns to turn to Taylor, who responded with a couple of 100-yard games during the final month as Texas finished unbeaten in the regular season for the first time since 1983.

Taylor got his first start at tailback against Baylor and ran for 102 yards and three touchdowns in a 62–0 win. Two weeks later, Taylor rushed for 102 yards and two more touchdowns in a 40–29 victory over Texas A&M.

In four starts, Taylor averaged 15 carries and 86 yards. During a four-game stretch late in the season, he accounted for 10 touchdowns.

"He could be," Brown said when asked if Taylor has the chance to be the next Bush. "It's a tough comparison because Reggie just won the Heisman and is arguably the best running back in college football."

freshman-debut record. With Selvin Young bothered by a nagging ankle injury early in the season, Charles made his first career start against Rice in Week 3 and had 189 yards and three touchdowns, the second-best rushing performance by a freshman in school history.

Charles, who entered the national title game with 844 yards, etched his name into Red River Shootout lore with an 80-yard touchdown run against Oklahoma, helping the Longhorns snap a five-game

The Longhorns could also pound the ball inside when they so desired, as 270-pound true freshman Henry Melton provided 10 touchdowns.

And it doesn't hurt to have a quarterback who can beat you with his legs as well as his arm. Vince Young led the Longhorns during the regular season with 850 yards rushing and added nine scores of his own, as Texas piled up an amazing 50 touchdowns on the ground. ■

PITTMAN LEADS BIG-PLAY RECEIVING CORPS

AUSTIN, Texas – Good luck runs in Billy Pittman's family.

So does bad luck.

In 2003, Pittman's grandmother, Gwen Kelley, won a $1.5 million Texas Two-Step lottery jackpot. That same year, Pittman began experiencing a rash of injuries that threatened to derail his UT career before it ever started.

"It was so frustrating. I could have easily quit," said Pittman, a sophomore receiver for the second-ranked Texas Longhorns. "I didn't know if I wanted to keep playing."

Some of the injuries were the typical aches and pains: torn quadriceps in both legs, a separated AC joint in his left shoulder. None of it compared to the morning during his freshman year when Pittman woke up with his eye twitching, the left side of his face paralyzed and an inability to speak properly.

Doctors diagnosed him with Bell's palsy and told him he might never be the same again.

A month later, things returned to normal. Finally free of the injuries that briefly postponed the start of his college career, Pittman emerged as one of the Longhorns' go-to receivers this season, leading the team with 697 yards and a nation-best 23.2 yards-per-catch to earn honorable mention All-Big 12 honors

"A lot of kids would have given up," Texas coach Mack Brown said of Pittman. "He had every bad thing happen to him that you could think of."

Entering the season, the Longhorns did not have a player returning who caught a touchdown a year ago. UT had eight receivers combine for 114 receptions, 2,012 yards and 16 touchdowns in 12 games.

Pittman saved some of his best performances for the Longhorns' biggest games. His breakout game of the season came in Week 2 in a highly anticipated showdown with fourth-ranked Ohio State. Pittman caught five passes for 130 yards, including a five-yard touchdown, as the Longhorns beat the Buckeyes 25–22.

Pittman had four receptions for 100 yards and two touchdowns to help the Longhorns snap a five-year losing streak to archrival Oklahoma in early October. His 64-yard touchdown just before half-time was the backbreaker, putting Texas ahead 24–6. In the third quarter, he made a spectacular one-handed catch on a 27-yard touchdown.

Two weeks later, he followed with 138 yards and two touchdowns in a blowout of No. 10 Texas Tech. He just missed another 100-yard game against Colorado by one yard. The three 100-yard games by Pittman were the most since Williams had four in 2003.

Pittman and quarterback Vince Young connected for four plays of 60 yards or longer this season.

"I don't really think much of it," Pittman said. "I just happen to get the ball in the big games."

After a rough start to his college career, Pittman is just happy to be on the football field. ∎

Pittman has emerged from injury and adversity to be one of Vince Young's go-to receivers.

"The message we're sending to our team in everything we do – from our off-season workouts to spring practice to the fall – is we want to go back to the Rose Bowl, and we want to win."

– Mack Brown prior to the 2005 season, on his team's prospects for the National Championship

MACK BROWN

Mack Brown has led the Longhorns' return to glory by doing things the way he's always done them: with an infectious enthusiasm, a commitment to excellence and an unmatched ability to amass talented players and motivate them to do great things – all in the context of a team-first family approach. In the process, he has restored the luster to the Longhorn tradition and rekindled the passion of America's greatest fans.

Brown has been a college head coach for 21 seasons. Before coming to Austin, he had turned North Carolina from double-digit losers (1–10 in both 1988 and '89) into a headliner on the national stage, compiling a record of 20–3 in 1996 and '97. Meanwhile, in Texas, the Longhorns had dipped to 4–7 in 1997, but Brown came to the rescue in 1998. In his first year on the job, he turned in a 9–3 record and a 15th-place ranking in the final AP poll.

Four out of Brown's last five teams have finished in the Top 10. On New Year's Day, 2005, Brown's Longhorns scored a 38–37 Rose Bowl win over Big Ten champion Michigan. Many suspected then that that game was simply a prelude to a return trip with even bigger stakes; they were right.

Brown's seven-year record at Texas (heading into the 2006 Rose Bowl) stands at 82–19, for a winning percentage of .812.

Mack Brown Year-by-Year at Texas

Year	Record	Bowl Game
1998	9–3	Cotton
1999	9–5	Cotton
2000	9–3	Holiday
2001	11–2	Holiday
2002	11–2	Cotton
2003	10–3	Holiday
2004	11–1	Rose
2005	13-0	Rose

"Coach Brown's enthusiasm for the game of football is what makes him a great coach. It's evident by the coaches he's brought in and also by the enthusiasm his players show. That enthusiasm transcends all the way from the head coach and the assistants to the players and ultimately the fans."

— Major Applewhite, former Longhorns quarterback

"We have taken dead aim all season and it is good to be back here in Los Angeles playing for the National Championship."

— Brown, in the days before the Rose Bowl

Mack Brown has quietly orchestrated one of the greatest runs in Texas football history.

"Mack has become one of my good friends. People tell me, 'Well, he reminds me a lot of you.' And I say, 'I have not seen a single thing done the wrong way.' And I see a lot of things that he's doing that I could have learned from."

– Legendary Longhorns head coach Darrell Royal

Texas head football coach Mack Brown applauds his team after a touchdown during first quarter action against Texas Tech.

THIS IS TEXAS FOOTBALL

The sights and sounds of Game Day in Austin create an unmatched spectacle, a glorious mix of tradition and color and pomp and pageantry. Here's a small sample of what makes Texas football unique.

The colors and nickname

They're as familiar to Texas fans as the Lone Star on the state flag – the Longhorns, clad in burnt orange and white.

The University of Texas began playing football in 1893 with gold and white as its colors, and the nickname of "Varsity." In 1900, the University's Board of Regents officially declared the school's colors to be orange and white. Three years later, Daily Texan sportswriter D.A. Frank referred to the team as Longhorns. After years of continuous usage, the unofficial moniker became the team's official nickname.

Bevo

The University of Texas students were presented with a Longhorn steer at halftime of the 1916 Texas A&M game by a group led by Stephen Pinckney, a UT alum and official with the U.S. Attorney General's office. Ever since then, the lean, tenacious animal has been the school's mascot. There are conflicting accounts regarding the origin of his name, including one that involves a non-alcoholic near beer named Bevo that was on the market at that time. Another version has some Aggies kidnapping the steer

after their loss to Texas in 1916 and branding it with the 13–0 score of the 1915 game, which A&M had won. Upon the animal's return, some enterprising Texas students changed the 13 to a B, the dash to an E, inserted a V and left the O as it was – BEVO. The most likely explanation is that Bevo is a play on the word "beeve," a slang term that means "steer" and was in common usage in the Southwest in the early decades of the 20th century. By the way, Texas won that 1916 Texas A&M contest with the Aggies 21–7.

Hook 'em Horns

Texas cheerleader Harley Clark instituted the Hook 'em Horns hand signal at a pep rally preceding the 1955 TCU game. Henry Pitts, a University of Texas student, was the one who actually came up with the gesture, symbolizing Longhorn mascot Bevo's horns, as a shadow casting idea. Pitts shared his inspiration with Clark, and at the game against the Horned Frogs on Saturday, Texas lost 40–27 but saw the birth of an institution, as the Hook 'em Horns signal surged repeatedly from one end of the stadium to the other.

The Showband of the Southwest

The University of Texas marching band was founded in 1900, before the football team was called the Longhorns, and the same year the Board of Regents declared the school colors to be orange and white. Chemistry professor Dr. E.P. Schoch, in an effort to drum up campus-wide interest in the football

team, raised $150 to purchase instruments from Jackson's Pawn Shop in Austin and collected a group of 16 musicians to add to the excitement at Clark Field on fall Saturdays. From those humble beginnings, what later became known as the Showband of the Southwest was born.

Dr. H.E. Baxter was the band's first director, and served in that capacity for five years. Under the directorship of Colonel George E. Hurt from 1937 to 1949, the band grew to over 200 members. The band currently encompasses 360 members, and although it requires a year-round commitment as a course offered by the School of Music, many different academic disciplines are represented.

As pregame excitement builds to a fever pitch in Royal-Memorial Stadium, the stands bulging with over 80,000 spectators, the band explodes out of the tunnel in perfect formation, following the world's largest bass drum – Big Bertha – onto the field, all hands raised in the "hook 'em" sign. The Longhorn

Band then plays "Deep in the Heart of Texas," and covers half the field with a giant block-T as 900 pounds and 777 square yards of Texas state flag are unfurled over the other half of the field. The football team then enters the playing field through the T.

The Showband of the Southwest has marched at presidential inauguration parades, inspiring a "hook 'em" sign from President George W. Bush in 2001. In 1986, it was awarded the Sudler Trophy, recognizing the top university marching band in the nation. Many of the band members also participate in any one or more of three concert bands, two jazz ensembles and a basketball-game pep band.

Big Bertha

The largest bass drum in the world – Big Bertha – belongs to the University of Texas' marching band. Although she has been a staple of the Longhorn Band performances since 1955, Big Bertha is actually more than 80 years old. She was actually built for the

University of Chicago and was first used in the Chicago-Princeton game in 1922. After a period of inactivity subsequent to the Maroons' discontinuing their football program, Colonel D. Harold Byrd purchased Bertha for the Longhorn Band.

Big Bertha is eight feet in diameter and 54 inches wide, and when mounted on her trailer, she stands over 10 feet tall. Prior to each game in Royal-Memorial Stadium, a group of students known as the "Bertha Crew" rolls the giant drum onto the field ahead of the Showband of the Southwest, and the stadium crowd erupts. During games Big Bertha is stationed in the end zone, where she greets every Longhorn score with loud booming while being spun around by the crew.

The UT Tower

The 27-story UT Tower serves not only as the Main Building on the Austin campus, but it also heralds the football team's great triumphs. For all regular-season victories other than Texas A&M, and all non-BCS bowl wins, the building is lit orange on top with a white shaft. For wins over Texas A&M, and Big 12 Conference and South Division titles, the tower is lit up entirely in orange. A Longhorns national championship finds an all-orange lighting with a #1 display.

Darrell K Royal-Texas Memorial Stadium

In the days leading up to the Thanksgiving Day, 1923, game with Texas A&M, Texas athletic director Theo Bellmont began openly campaigning for a concrete stadium to replace Clark Field as a home football venue. Plans were drawn up and the facility was completed in record time. The stadium, with a seating capacity of 27,000, was dedicated on Thanksgiving Day, 1924, with the Longhorns defeating the Aggies 7–0. The student body, which had been instrumental along with Bellmont in turning the stadium from an idea to a reality, decided it must be dedicated to the veterans from the state of

Texas who had fought in World War I.

In 1926 the north end was closed in, creating a horseshoe and increasing seating capacity to 40,500. Subsequent expansions have brought the stands to their current capacity of 80,082. For 27 years, beginning in 1969, the playing surface was Astro Turf, until it was removed following the 1995 season and replaced with Prescription Athletic turf. The PAT in turn was replaced in 2002 with Bermudagrass.

In 1996 the stadium was rededicated to honor the memory of all American war veterans. Also that year, the name of Darrell K Royal, the coach who brought three national titles to the University of Texas, was added to that of the stadium.

National Championships
1963 (AP, UPI)

Coach Darrell Royal's 1963 Texas team opened the campaign with a No. 5 national ranking and quickly shot to the top. After resounding victories in games 1 and 2, the Longhorns found themselves at No. 2 in the nation. They held firm in that spot after a 34–7 win over Oklahoma State, setting up the annual battle with Oklahoma in Dallas. The Sooners were the nation's top-ranked team going in, but the Horns took the top spot from them with a 28–7 victory. The biggest play of the season might have come four weeks later in the Baylor game. Duke Carlisle saved Texas' season that day with a sensational leaping interception of a potential game-tying touchdown pass from Baylor's Don Trull to Lawrence Elkins with 29 seconds left. The Texas A&M contest was another white-knuckler – a 15–13 victory after trailing the Aggies 13–3 to start the fourth quarter. Carlisle scored the winning touchdown with 1:19 to play. The finishing touch on the title was a 28–6 Cotton Bowl victory over second-ranked Navy, quarterbacked by that year's Heisman winner, Roger Staubach. Carlisle connected with Phil Harris on touchdown passes of 58 and 63 yards in the win. Tommy Ford led the

"The Eyes of Texas"
"The eyes of Texas are upon you all the live long day …
The eyes of Texas are upon you, you cannot get away …
Do not think you can escape them at night or early in the morn …
The eyes of Texas are upon you 'til Gabriel blows his horn."

"Texas Fight"
Texas Fight, Texas Fight,
And it's goodbye to A&M.
Texas Fight, Texas Fight,
And we'll put over one more win.
Texas Fight, Texas Fight,
For it's Texas that we love the best.
Give 'em hell! Give 'em hell!
Go Horns, Go!
(YELL)
Yea Orange! Yea White!
Yea Longhorns! Fight! Fight! Fight!
Texas Fight! Texas Fight!
Yea Texas Fight!
Texas Fight! Texas Fight!
Yea Texas Fight!
(repeat chorus)

Longhorns' 1963 rushing attack with 763 yards; tackle Scott Appleton was a consensus All-American and won the Outland Trophy. Linebacker Tommy Nobis enjoyed a sensational sophomore campaign, two years before winning the 1965 Maxwell Award as the nation's outstanding player.

1969 (AP, UPI)

Just as in 1963, Texas' 1969 national title campaign involved a No. 1 vs. No. 2 matchup. This time Arkansas was the opponent in a game that ABC-TV

No one is happier about Texas' remarkable 2005 season than the legendary Darrell Royal.

had moved from Oct. 18 to Dec. 5. It took an assist from Michigan, which defeated top-ranked Ohio State on Nov. 22, to vault the Longhorns over the Buckeyes to the top spot in the polls. A 15–14 Texas win over the second-ranked Razorbacks in the regular-season finale followed by a 21–17 Cotton Bowl victory over Notre Dame left little doubt among fans and pollsters as to who the champion of college football was that year. A spotless 11–0 record didn't hurt, either.

Any list of "Games of the Century" that does not include the 1969 Texas-Arkansas game is of no interest. UT quarterback James Street ran for a touchdown and a two-point conversion that day, and connected with receiver Randy Peschel on a crucial 4th-and-3 play late in the game. In the victors' locker room following the game, President Richard Nixon awarded the Texas team a plaque emblematic of the National Championship.

On New Year's Day, Texas trailed coach Ara Parseghian's Fighting Irish 17–14 midway through the fourth quarter when Street piloted the Longhorns 76 yards to the winning score, with Billy Dale doing the honors from one yard out.

All season long, Street masterfully guided the wishbone offense, then in its second year of existence. The 1969 Longhorns led the nation in rushing with 363 yards per contest. In the SMU game, the Horns rushed for 611 yards, with Street, halfbacks Jim Bertelsen and Ted Koy, and fullback Steve Worster each surpassing the century mark. Worster, wide receiver Cotton Speyrer, linebacker Glen Halsell and tackles Bob McKay and Bobby Wuensch were All-Americans.

1970 (UPI)

Texas entered the 1970 season defending a national championship and sitting on a 20-game winning streak, yet were ranked second nationally and remained there until claiming the top spot in late October. It took a game-winning, 45-yard

Conference Championships (26)

Year	Conference	Overall
1920	5–0–0 (SWC)	9–0–0
1928	5–1–0 (SWC)	7–2–0
1930	4–1–0 (SWC)	8–1–1
1942	5–1–0 (SWC)	9–2–0
1943	5–0–0 (SWC)	7–1–1
1945	5–1–0 (SWC)	10–1–0
1950	6–0–0 (SWC)	9–2–0
1952	6–0–0 (SWC)	9–2–0
*1953	5–1–0 (SWC)	7–3–0
*1959	5–1–0 (SWC)	9–2–0
*1961	6–1–0 (SWC)	10–1–0
1962	6–0–1 (SWC)	9–1–1
1963	7–0–0 (SWC)	11–0–0
*1968	6–1–0 (SWC)	9–1–1
1969	7–0–0 (SWC)	11–0–0
1970	7–0–0 (SWC)	10–1–0
1971	6–1–0 (SWC)	8–3–0
1972	7–0–0 (SWC)	10–1–0
1973	7–0–0 (SWC)	8–3–0
*1975	6–1–0 (SWC)	10–2–0
1977	8–0–0 (SWC)	11–1–0
1983	8–0–0 (SWC)	11–1–0
1990	8–0–0 (SWC)	10–2–0
*1994	4–3–0 (SWC)	8–4–0
1995	7–0–0 (SWC)	10–2–1
1996	6–2–0 (Big 12)	8–5–0
2005	8–0–0 (Big 12)	12–0

*co-championships

touchdown pass from quarterback Eddie Phillips to Cotton Speyrer with 12 seconds remaining against 13th-ranked UCLA to pull out a 20–17 win and extend the Longhorns' winning streak to 23.

The following week, Texas pounded Oklahoma 49–9. That win and the 45–21 victory over Rice the following week promoted the Horns to No. 1, a position they never relinquished. The regular season concluded with blowout victories over Texas A&M (52–14) and fourth-ranked Arkansas (42–7).

The 1970 Texas team had ridden its wishbone

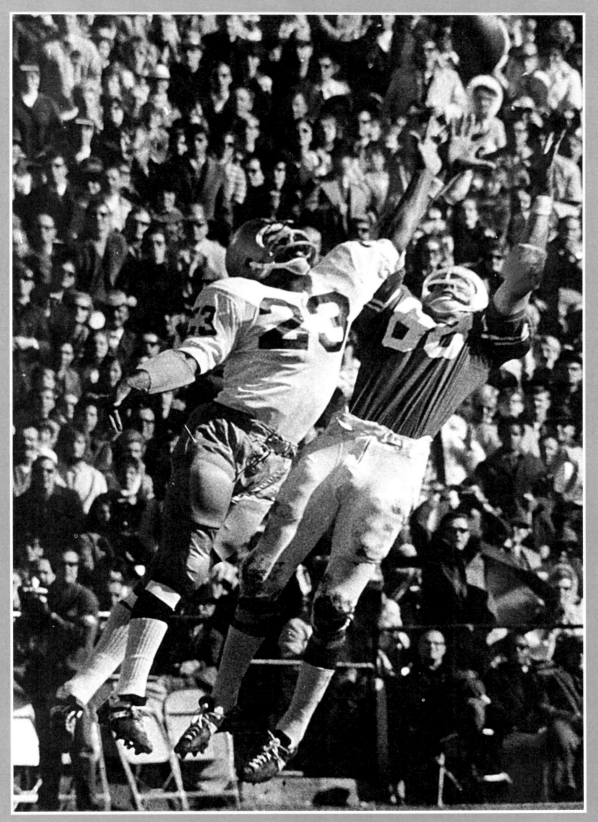

The 1970 seniors ended their college careers with a sparkling 30-2-1 record.

> **"Earl Campbell is the greatest football player I have ever seen, and Ann Campbell (Earl's mother and inspiration) is the best coach there ever was!"**
> — Texas coach Fred Akers, after Campbell's 173-yard performance against Houston despite suffering from the flu

offense to a 10–0 mark, a third consecutive Southwest Conference championship and a date with ninth-ranked Notre Dame in the Cotton Bowl. The Irish stopped Texas winning streak at 30 games on New Year's Day, 1971, and dropped the Longhorns to No. 3 in the AP poll. But the UPI poll was closed after the regular season, locking Texas in as national champion.

The 1970 Longhorns outdid themselves, topping the previous season's incredible rushing output with a still-standing school record 374.5 yards per game on the ground. Fullback Steve Worster, wide receiver Cotton Speyrer, offensive tackle Bobby Wuensch, defensive end Bill Atessis and linebacker Scott Henderson were All-Americans. The "Worster crowd," the fabulous freshmen class of 1967, concluded their college careers with a record of 30–2–1.

Longhorn Legends

Texas' roster of greats reads like a who's who of college football legends. The names are familiar to fans of college football, and for the fans of Texas' rivals, they still bring a shiver of dread. Here are some of the stars who have shone brightest during their tenures in Austin.

Cedric Benson, Running Back, 2001-04

In 2004, Benson passed Earl Campbell into second place on UT's career rushing list with 5,540 yards, second only to Ricky Williams' 6.279, Benson's 64 career rushing touchdowns are also second-most in school history. He ran for over 1,000 yards all four years of his college career – 1,053 as a freshman, 1,293 as a sophomore, 1,306 as a junior, and 1,834 (third on the UT single-season charts) as a senior. Also as a senior, he cap-

tured the Doak Walker Award as the nation's best running back.

Earl Campbell, Tailback, 1974-77

As a freshman, Campbell ran for 928 yards playing fullback in coach Darrell Royal's wishbone offense. Fred Akers replaced Royal as coach in 1977 and made Campbell the deep back in the I-formation. Campbell became Texas' first Heisman Trophy winner that year, when he rushed for 1,744 yards (a Southwest Conference record that stood for 16 years) and 19 touchdowns. He led the nation in rushing and scoring that fall and set a UT record with 10 100-yard games. Campbell is a member of both the College and Pro Football Halls of Fame.

Derrick Johnson, Linebacker, 2001-04

If Johnson isn't the greatest linebacker in Texas football history, he certainly ranks right up there with Tommy Nobis. Johnson was big, fast, explosive and instinctive. In 2001 he was national Freshman of the Year. He was consensus first-team All-Big 12 each of the next three years and consensus first-team All-America as a junior and senior. In 2004 he won the Butkus Award as the nation's best linebacker and the Nagurski Award as the nation's best defensive player. Over his career he recorded 458 total tackles, 65 tackles for loss, 30 pass breakups and nine interceptions.

Bobby Layne, Quarterback, 1944-47

Layne is generally regarded as not only the greatest quarterbacks in Texas history, but also one of the greatest of all time. He entered the university on scholarship to play baseball – he was an accom-

The Tyler Rose terrorized defenses on his way to the 1977 Heisman Trophy.

"I'd rather play against Dick Butkus than Nobis."

— Dolphins running back Larry Csonka

plished pitcher — but it wasn't long before coach Dana X. Bible recruited him to throw the football as well. He completed 210 of 400 passes for 3,145 yards over his college career. He saved some of his best performances for the postseason, lighting up the scoreboard in the Longhorns' 40–27 victory over Missouri (when he accounted for all 40 of his team's points by running, passing, and kicking) in the 1946 Cotton Bowl, and the 27–7 victory over sixth-ranked Alabama in the 1948 Sugar Bowl. His stellar 15-year career in the NFL included three league titles. Layne is an enshrinee in both the College and Pro Football Halls of Fame.

Roosevelt Leaks, Running Back, 1972-74

As a junior in 1973, Leaks finished third in Heisman Trophy voting, the highest finish on record for a UT underclassman. That year he became the first African-American All-American in the school's history after setting the Southwest Conference single-season rushing record with 1,415 yards, averaging 6.2 per carry. A serious knee injury hampered his senior season and professional career — he played nine years for the Baltimore Colts and Buffalo Bills. He still ranks fifth on the Texas career rushing chart, and he is a member of the 2005 class of College Football Hall of Fame inductees.

Tommy Nobis, Linebacker-Guard, 1963-65

Tommy Nobis is one of the greatest linebackers who ever lived, and he also played a mean offensive guard as a two-way college standout. He was a three-time All-Southwest Conference honoree and a two-time All-American. He was the only sophomore starter on coach Darrell Royal's 1963 national champion Longhorn team. In the Orange Bowl fol-

lowing his junior season, he registered perhaps the most meaningful tackle in school history, stopping Alabama quarterback Joe Namath at the goal line on fourth and inches and saving the 21–17 win for Texas. As a senior, he won both the Outland Trophy and Maxwell Award, averaging almost 20 tackles per game. In the 1966 NFL Draft, he was the No. 1 overall pick by the Atlanta Falcons' expansion franchise, where he earned NFL Rookie of the Year honors in 1966 and was voted to five Pro Bowls. His ongoing absence from the Pro Football Hall of Fame is a glaring omission.

Darrell Royal, Head Coach, 1957-76

A coach doesn't get a magnificent football stadium named after him unless he's achieved legendary status, and Darrell Royal, whose name was affixed to that of Texas Memorial Stadium in 1996, qualifies as a legend. Royal is the winningest coach in University of Texas history.

After bottoming out at 1–9 in 1956, Texas hired Royal, the former Oklahoma halfback and Mississippi State and Washington head coach, and he produced a 6–4–1 mark right off the bat. In 20 years at Austin, from 1957-1976, Royal compiled a record of 167–47–5. During the seasons of 1968 through 1970, his teams won 30 games in a row.

Royal's Longhorns captured 11 Southwest Conference titles and were national champions three times — in 1963, 1969 and 1970. He coached 77 all-conference players and 26 All-Americans.

Ricky Williams, Running Back, 1995-98

In 1995, Williams started at fullback as a true freshman and broke Earl Campbell's school freshman record with 990 yards. As a senior tailback in 1998,

Bobby Layne went from Texas legend to NFL icon during his unparalleled career.

Williams seized the NCAA career rushing record in dramatic fashion, with a dazzling 60-yard touchdown run against Texas A&M. He was a two-time All-American and the first player ever to win the Doak Walker Award twice (1997 and '98). His senior year, when he rushed for a school single-season record 2,124 yards, he was named AP Player of the Year and Walter Camp Player of the Year, and won the Maxwell Award and the Heisman Trophy. He averaged 6.2 yards per carry for his career, and his 6,279 rushing yards still ranks second in NCAA history.

Talkin' Texas Football

We thought we'd go straight to the source and let some of Texas' greatest legends share their thoughts about Longhorn football. They put it much better than we could.

"I never went bear-huntin' with a switch."
— Darrell Royal, on his habit of recruiting great players to play at Texas

"I'm not a football fan, but I am a fan of people, and I am a Darrell Royal fan because he is the rarest of human beings."
— Former president Lyndon Johnson

"When I got ready for Arkansas, I was like the players. We were p———- off, and we stayed that way until the game was over. It's just a frame of mind. You know, the leaves up there turn earlier in the fall. We'd be on the bus, and I'd notice the leaves, or see a Hog bumper sticker, and get p———- off. I had on my gameface."
— Darrell Royal, on the rivalry with Arkansas (Athlon Southwest Football, 1979)

"Earl Campbell is the secret. Coaches who have an Earl Campbell know the secret. Those who don't have an Earl Campbell, don't."
— Darrell Royal, on the impetus behind Texas' undefeated 1977 regular season

"And now, the moment we've been waiting for: The award for the most outstanding college football player in America goes to Earl Campbell."
— The first Heisman winner, Jay Berwanger, at the Downtown Athletic Club's Heisman Trophy award ceremony, 1977

"Mack Brown's like the Darrell Royal of the 21st century. He's hard-working and has great concern for his athletes. The coaches and players work hard and support one another, and that's exactly how Coach Royal ran things."
— Jerry Sisemore, Texas All-American and All-Pro offensive tackle

"You've never played in an all-out, fight-for-your-life, backyard brawl rivalry until you've played in a Texas-Texas A&M game. It's an experience you will never forget."
— Texas All-Big 12 defensive lineman Shaun Rogers

"Honestly, I don't think there's anything better in this world than being an athlete at the University of Texas."
— Record-setting Longhorn QB Chris Simms

"I'm looking forward to being out there in my Texas jersey with all of the guys for one more year."
— Running back Cedric Benson, announcing that he would return for his senior season

"We want our linemen to run like our linebackers. We want our linebackers to run like our DBs and wide receivers. And we want our running backs, wide receivers and DBs to run like the fastest men in the world."
— Texas strength coach Jeff "Mad Dog" Madden

Run, Ricky, run: Ricky Williams produced his best football at the biggest moments.

"I m ready to go to Dallas and stick my chest out and bump into as many OU folks as I can this October. With our big boys up front, this is our year. It s time for Mack Brown to start a streak of his own."

– Kenneth Sims, 1981 Lombardi Trophy winner and top pick in the 1982 NFL Draft (Dallas Morning News - 2005)

SIDELINE SPIRIT

What takes place on fall afternoons in the storied confines of Darrell K Royal-Texas Memorial Stadium is more than simply a game; it's a way of life. If you've experienced the passion of thousands of UT fans with hands thrust skyward flashing the familiar "Hook 'em Horns" sign, you know exactly what we're talking about. In 2005, we've witnessed a season-long celebration of that passion.

Longhorn legend Tommy Nobis puts it best: "On game days at Texas, you get a fresh new sense of Texas pride throughout the stadium when they give the Hook 'em Horns sign and sing 'The Eyes of Texas' … The team, the faculty, the students, the alumni and the community are united together as family."

And once you're part of the Longhorn family, you never leave.

"I'm still burning orange."
— Priest Holmes, Texas running back and NFL All-Pro

"You can't help but stand up and put up the Horns sign when they play 'The Eyes of Texas.' It takes you over. Whether you're in Orlando, Columbus, Detroit, Ann Arbor or wherever, you stand up and it gets into your heart and soul."
— ESPN's Lee Corso

While USC's Reggie Bush squeezed in for a spectacular fourth-quarter score in the Rose Bowl, Michael Huff and the Texas defense held the 2005 Heisman Trophy winner in check for most of the championship game.

AP Wide World

Longhorns Football

Passing Statistics

NAME	CMP	ATT	YDS	CMP%	YDS/A	TD	INT	RAT
Vince Young	182	285	2769	63.9	9.72	26	10	168.6
Matt Nordgren	6	11	47	54.5	4.27	0	1	72.3
Totals	188	296	2816	63.5	9.51	26	11	165.0

Rushing Statistics

NAME	CAR	YDS	YPC	LONG	TD
Vince Young	136	850	6.3	80(TD)	9
Jamaal Charles	114	844	7.4	80(TD)	11
Ramonce Taylor	72	501	7.0	57(TD)	11
Henry Melton	87	432	5.0	27	10
Selvin Young	89	416	4.7	28	7
Chris Ogbonnaya	22	76	3.5	22(TD)	1
Matt Nordgren	12	38	3.2	11	1
Matthew McCoy	6	31	5.2	25	0
Billy Pittman	2	28	14.0	19	0
Antwan Hobbs	9	27	3.0	12	0
Michael Houston	2	25	12.5	14	0
Scott Ballew	4	14	3.5	9	0
Ahmard Hall	1	10	10.0	10	0
Rashad Bobino	1	6	6.0	6	0
Marcus Myers	4	5	1.3	3	0
Scott Derry	1	2	2.0	2	0
Totals	569	3285	5.8	80	50

Receiving Statistics

NAME	REC	YDS	YPR	LONG	TD
Billy Pittman	30	697	23.2	75(TD)	5
David Thomas	40	525	13.1	32	5
Limas Sweed	28	480	17.1	45(TD)	5
Ramonce Taylor	25	268	10.7	42(TD)	3
Quan Cosby	13	254	19.5	64(TD)	2
Brian Carter	15	211	14.1	40	0
Jamaal Charles	14	157	11.2	36	2
Nate Jones	9	67	7.4	14	1
Neale Tweedie	2	49	24.5	28	1
Ahmard Hall	3	42	14.0	25	1
Selvin Young	4	25	6.3	14	0
George Walker	1	22	22.0	22	0
Tyrell Gatewood	2	13	6.5	9	0
Chris Ogbonnaya	1	3	3.0	3	0
Peter Ullman	1	3	3.0	3(TD)	1
Totals	188	2816	15.0	75	26

Kicking Statistics

NAME	XPM	XPA	XP%	FGM	FGA	FG%	1-19	20-29	30-39	40-49	50+	LNG	PTS
David Pino	68	72	94.4	12	15	80	0/0	4/4	3/5	5/5	0/1	45	104
Richmond McGee	4	5	80	0	0	0	0/0	0/0	0/0	0/0	0/0	0	4
Kyle Phillips	1	1	100	0	0	0	0/0	0/0	0/0	0/0	0/0	0	1

2005 Award Winners

PLAYER	AWARD
Vince Young	Davey O'Brien Award
Michael Huff	Jim Thorpe Award
Vince Young	Maxwell Award

Overall Team Statistics · All games

TEAM STATISTICS	UT	OPP
SCORING	611	175
Points Per Game	50.9	14.6
FIRST DOWNS.	291	194
Rushing	165	94
Passing	107	84
Penalty	19	16
RUSHING YARDAGE	3285	1493
Yards gained rushing	3550	1885
Yards lost rushing	265	392
Rushing Attempts	569	420
Average Per Rush	5.8	3.6
Average Per Game	273.8	124.4
TDs Rushing	50	11
PASSING YARDAGE	2816	1871
Att-Comp-Int	296-188-11	395-194-10
Average Per Pass	9.5	4.7
Average Per Catch	15.0	9.6
Average Per Game	234.7	155.9
TDs Passing	26	9
TOTAL OFFENSE	6101	3364
Total Plays	865	815
Average Per Play.	7.1	4.1
Average Per Game	508.4	280.3
KICK RETURNS: #-YARDS	21-564	73-1392
PUNT RETURNS: #-YARDS	41-652	10-70
INT RETURNS: #-YARDS	10-90	11-151
KICK RETURN AVERAGE	26.9	19.1
PUNT RETURN AVERAGE	15.9	7.0
INT RETURN AVERAGE	9.0	13.7
FUMBLES-LOST	31-8	26-15
PENALTIES-YARDS	95-818	101-815
Average Per Game	68.2	67.9
PUNTS-YARDS	36-1376	87-3402
Average Per Punt	38.2	39.1
Net punt average	36.3	31.6
TIME OF POSSESSION/GAM	31:08	28:52
3RD-DOWN CONVERSIONS	83/162	53/186
3rd-Down Pct.	51%	28%
4TH-DOWN CONVERSIONS	11/18	9/18
4th-Down Pct.	61%	50%
SACKS BY-YARDS	31-253	14-102
MISC YARDS	97	0
TOUCHDOWNS SCORED	83	20
FIELD GOALS-ATTEMPTS	12-15	13-19
PAT-ATTEMPTS	73-81	16-17
ATTENDANCE	416,663	342,231
Games/Avg Per Game	5/83,333	5/68,446
Neutral Site Game	2/73,280	

SCORE BY QUARTERS	1st	2nd	3rd	4th	Total
Texas	160	202	151	98	611
Opponents	59	45	44	27	175

2005 Roster

NUMBER	NAME	HT.	WT.	CLASS	POS.	HOMETOWN
72	Will Allen	6'6"	315	Sr.-3L	OG	Houston, TX (Cypress Falls)
47	Steven Andrade*	6'2"	225	Sr.-SQ	DE	San Antonio, TX (Southwest)
12	Sam Areias*	5'7"	201	Jr.-SQ	RB	Los Banos, CA (Los Banos)
82	Coy Aune*	6'2"	195	So.-SQ	WR	Austin, TX (Westlake)
39	Ryan Bailey*	6'2"	180	Fr.-HS	K/P	Austin, TX (Anderson)
63	Justin Blalock	6'4"	329	Jr.-2L	OT	Plano, TX (East)
44	Rashad Bobino	5'11"	230	Fr.-RS	LB	West Texas City, TX (LaMarque)
35	Todd Bondy*	6'0"	210	So.-SQ	LB	Southlake, TX (Carroll)
5	Tarell Brown	6'0"	200	Jr.-2L	CB	Mesquite, TX (North Mesquite)
48	Christopher Brown	6'3"	210	Fr.-HS	LB/DE	Texarkana, TX (Texas)
18	Will Buchanan*	6'1"	180	Fr.-HS	QB	Austin, TX (Austin)
43	Jeremy Campbell	6'2"	220	Fr.-RS	LB	Richardson, TX (Lake Highlands)
19	Benjamin Campos*	5'10"	192	Jr.-SQ	PK	New Braunfels, TX (New Braunfels)
2	Brian Carter	5'11"	190	Sr.-2L	WR	The Woodlands, TX (The Woodlands)
23	Jaime Carvajal*	5'4"	147	So.-SQ	RB	Taft, TX (Taft)
17	Xang Chareunsab*	5'8"	155	Sr.-SQ	WR	Houston, TX (Aldine MacArthur)
25	Jamaal Charles	6'1"	190	Fr.-HS	RB	Port Arthur, TX (Memorial)
6	Quan Cosby	5'11"	200	Fr.-HS	WR	Mart, TX (Mart)
80	Tim Crowder	6'4"	270	Jr.-2L	DE	Tyler, TX (John Tyler)
33	Scott Derry	6'3"	230	So.-1L	LB	Pearland, TX (Pearland)
92	Larry Dibbles	6'2"	285	Sr.-2L	DT	Lancaster, TX (Lancaster)
55	Cedric Dockery	6'4"	315	Fr.-RS	OG	Garland, TX (Lakeview Centennial)
70	Greg Dolan	6'7"	290	Fr.-RS	OT	Austin, TX (Westwood)
85	Jermichael Finley	6'5"	220	Fr.-HS	WR/TE	Diboll, TX (Diboll)
21	Michael Flath*	5'9"	180	So.-HS	S	Arcadia, CA (Arcadia)
21	Eric Foreman	6'4"	230	So.-1L	LB	Corrigan, TX (Camden)
28	Brandon Foster	5'9"	180	So.-SQ	CB	Arlington, TX (Bowie)
22	Adair Fragoso*	5'11"	215	Jr.-SQ	QB	El Paso, TX (Faith Christian Academy)
51	Mike Garcia	6'3"	315	Sr.-2L	OG	Houston, TX (Galena Park)
1	Tyrell Gatewood	6'2"	210	So.-SQ	TE/WR	Tyler, TX (Chapel Hill)
17	Trevor Gerland	6'2"	190	Fr.-HS	P	Katy, TX (Cinco Ranch)
8	Cedric Griffin	6'2"	205	Sr.-3L	CB	San Antonio, TX (Holmes)
67	Dallas Griffin	6'4"	275	So.-SQ	C	Katy, TX (Taylor)
26	Marcus Griffin	6'0"	195	So.-1L	S	Austin, TX (Bowie)
27	Michael Griffin	6'0"	205	Jr.-2L	S	Austin, TX (Bowie)
46	Ahmard Hall	5'11"	235	Sr.-1L	RB	Angleton, TX (Angleton)
49	Eric Hall	6'2"	245	Sr.-2L	DE	Clarksville, TN (Northwest)
71	Chris Hall	6'4"	280	Fr.-HS	OG	Irving, TX (Irving)
23	Myron Hardy	6'2"	210	So.-SQ	WR	Austin, TX (McNeil)
2	Aaron Harris	6'0"	230	Sr.-3L	LB	Mesquite, TX (North Mesquite)
58	William Harvey*	5'11"	212	Fr.-HS	DS	Houston, TX (Memorial)
79	Tony Hills	6'6"	295	So.-1L	OT	Houston, TX (Alief Elsik)
28	Antwaun Hobbs*	5'7"	180	Jr.-SQ	RB	Garland, TX (South Garland)
29	Matthew Hofer*	5'6"	165	So.-SQ	RB	Austin, TX (Austin)
83	Steven Hogan	6'5"	255	So.-SQ	TE	Sugar Land, TX (Strake Jesuit)
7	Michael Huff	6'1"	205	Sr.-3L	S/CB	Irving, TX (Nimitz)
13	Erick Jackson	6'2"	185	So.-SQ	CB	Cedar Hill, TX (Duncanville)
99	Kaelen Jakes	6'3"	270	Sr.-1L	DE	Valencia, CA (Valencia)
91	Tully Janszen	6'3"	280	Jr.-1L	DT	Keller, TX (Keller)
30	Braden Johnson	6'1"	200	Sr.-1L	LB	Euless, TX (Trinity)
97	Greg Johnson	6'1"	195	Jr.-TR	P/PK	Lilburn, GA (Parkview/Vanderbilt)
9	Nate Jones	6'2"	195	So.-1L	WR	Texarkana, TX (Texas)
4	Drew Kelson	6'2"	215	So.-1L	LB	Houston, TX (Lamar)
89	Daniel Kendall*	6'2"	185	Jr.-HS	WR	Houston, TX (George Bush)
40	Robert Killebrew	6'2"	230	So.-1L	LB	Spring, TX (Klein)
59	Chad Kugler*	6'2"	220	Fr.-HS	LB	Richardson, TX (Berkner)
26	Stephen Lane*	6'0"	185	Fr.-HS	RB	Tyler, TX (Gorman)
95	Aaron Lewis	6'4"	275	Fr.-HS	DE	Albuquerque, NM (La Cueva)
41	Matt Logan*	5'11"	156	Sr.-SQ	WR	Houston, TX (Jersey Village)
96	Derek Lokey	6'2"	275	So.-1L	DT	Denton, TX (Ryan)

Team Roster

NUMBER	NAME	HT.	WT.	CLASS	POS.	HOMETOWN
76	Thomas Marshall	6'6"	293	So.-SQ	DT	Dallas, TX (Bishop Dunne)
94	Marco Martin	6'3"	355	Jr.-SQ	DT	Mesquite, TX (Mesquite)
12	Colt McCoy	6'3"	195	Fr.-HS	QB	Tuscola, TX (Jim Ned)
25	Mark McCoy*	6'2"	188	Jr.-SQ	WR	Dallas, TX (Episcopal School of Dallas)
13	Matthew McCoy*	6'3"	195	Jr.-SQ	QB	Dallas, TX (Episcopal School of Dallas)
35	Richmond McGee	6'4"	203	Sr.-3L	P/PK	Garland, TX (Garland)
88	Mac McWhorter*	6'4"	226	Fr.-HS	TE	Austin, TX (Westwood)
3	Karim Meijer	5'10"	200	Sr.-1L	DB	Katy, TX (Taylor)
18	Matt Melton	6'0"	210	Jr.-2L	S	Flint, TX (Tyler-John Tyler)
37	Henry Melton	6'3"	270	Fr.-HS	RB	Grapevine, TX (Grapevine)
52	Cory Michner*	6'0"	210	Fr.-HS	DE	St. Louis, MO (Ladue)
75	Roy Miller	6'2"	300	Fr.-HS	DL	Killeen, TX (Shoemaker)
24	Ryan Moench*	6'0"	185	Fr.-HS	DB	Austin, TX (Westwood)
43	Justin Moore*	6'2"	185	Fr.-HS	P	Houston, TX (Jersey Village)
38	Roddrick Muckelroy	6'2"	230	Fr.-HS	LB	Hallsville, TX (Hallsville)
32	Marcus Myers	6'3"	250	Jr.-SQ	RB	Austin, TX (Connally)
7	Matt Nordgren	6'5"	235	Sr.-1L	QB	Dallas, TX (Bishop Lynch)
10	Ishie Oduegwu	5'10"	195	Fr.-HS	S	Denton, TX (Ryan)
3	Chris Ogbonnaya	6'1"	220	Fr.-RS	RB	Missouri City, TX (Strake Jesuit)
97	Frank Okam	6'5"	315	So.-1L	DT	Dallas, TX (Lake Highlands)
98	Brian Orakpo	6'4"	238	Fr.-RS	DE	Houston, TX (Lamar)
29	Ryan Palmer	5'10"	185	Fr.-RS	DB	Arlington, TX (Bowie)
57	Jason Perez*	5'8"	205	Sr.-SQ	LB	San Angelo, TX (Central)
46	Julian Peterman*	6'0"	200	Fr.-HS	LB	Schertz, TX (Clemens)
85	Christoph Peters*	6'3"	220	Jr.-HS	WR	Aachen, Germany
37	Kyle Phillips*	5'11"	192	Sr.-SQ	PK	Cypress, TX (Cy-Fair)
15	David Pino	5'8"	180	Sr.-2L	PK	Wichita Falls, TX (Rider)
5	Billy Pittman	6'0"	198	So.-SQ	WR	Cameron, TX (Yoe)
71	Brad Poronsky*	6'7"	290	Sr.-SQ	OT	Air Force Academy, CO (Air Academy)
86	Kirby Portley*	6'2"	232	Sr.-SQ	TE	Kilgore, TX (Kilgore)
36	James Ray*	5'9"	190	Sr.-SQ	DB	Hewitt, TX (Midway)
45	Nic Redwine	6'3"	225	Fr.-RS	LB/DE	Tyler, TX (Lee)
39	Brian Robison	6'3"	275	Jr.-2L	DE	Splendora, TX (Splendora)
31	Aaron Ross	6'1"	192	Jr.-2L	CB	Tyler, TX (John Tyler)
53	Nick Schroeder	6'2"	240	Sr.-1L	DS	The Woodlands, TX (The Woodlands)
48	Roberto Schuldes*	6'2"	200	Fr.-HS	LB	Modesto, CA (Modesto)
73	Jonathan Scott	6'7"	315	Sr.-3L	OT	Dallas, TX (Carter)
62	Lyle Sendlein	6'5"	305	Jr.-2L	C	Scottsdale, AZ (Chaparral)
8	Jordan Shipley	6'0"	184	Fr.-RS	WR	Burnet, TX (Burnet)
61	Jaicus Solis*	6'4"	250	Jr.-SQ	DT	San Angelo, TX (Grape Creek)
42	Cody Stavig*	5'10"	195	Sr.-SQ	DB	Clackamas, OR (Clackamas)
64	Kasey Studdard	6'3"	305	Jr.-1L	OG	Lone Tree, CO (Highlands Ranch)
4	Limas Sweed	6'5"	219	So.-1L	WR	Brenham, TX (Brenham)
52	Charlie Tanner	6'4"	280	Fr.-HS	C	Austin, TX (Anderson)
11	Ramonce Taylor	5'11"	195	So.-1L	RB/WR	Temple, TX (Belton)
54	Michael Taylor*	5'11"	219	Fr.-HS	C	West Texas City, TX (LaMarque)
27	Clayton Tefteller*	6'0"	175	Jr.-SQ	WR	Gilmer, TX (Gilmer)
16	David Thomas	6'3"	245	Sr.-3L	TE	Wolfforth, TX (Frenship)
50	Luke Tiemann*	6'2"	219	So.-HS	LB	Pflugerville, TX (Pflugerville)
14	Freddy Torres*	6'1"	190	Fr.-HS	QB	Pecos, TX (Pecos)
87	Neale Tweedie	6'5"	265	Jr.-2L	TE	Lucas, TX (Allen)
74	Adam Ulatoski	6'8"	290	Fr.-HS	OT	Southlake, TX (Carroll)
86	Peter Ullman	6'4"	252	Fr.-RS	TE	Austin, TX (Round Rock)
66	Brett Valdez	6'4"	305	Jr.-SQ	C	Brownwood, TX (Brownwood)
84	George Walker	6'3"	205	Fr.-RS	WR	Houston, TX (Westbury)
78	William Winston	6'7"	345	Sr.-3L	OT	Houston, TX (Madison)
90	Rodrique Wright	6'5"	315	Sr.-3L	DT	Houston, TX (Alief Hastings)
45	Jerren Wright*	5'10"	164	Sr.-SQ	DB	Houston, TX (Jersey Village)
22	Selvin Young	6'0"	215	Jr.-2L	RB	Houston, TX (Jersey Village)
10	Vince Young	6'5"	233	Jr.-2L	QB	Houston, TX (Madison)
16	Gilbert Zepeda*	6'0"	186	So.-SQ	QB	Pharr, TX (PSJA North)

*Non-scholarship player

Young won MVP honors for the second consecutive year in the Rose Bowl.

AP Wide World

AP Wide World

After winning the big one, Mack Brown celebrates with the championship trophy.